I0107480

ALA-UDEEN & THE MAGIC LAMP

# ALA-UDEEN
## & The
## Magic Lamp

IN RHYMED COUPLETS
WITH ILLUSTRATIONS

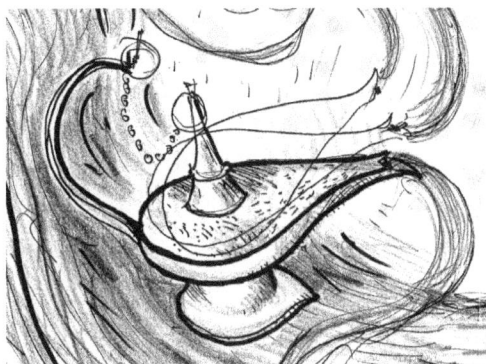

BY

## DANIEL ABDAL-HAYY MOORE

The Ecstatic Exchange
*Crescent Series*
2011
Philadelphia

Ala-udeen & the Magic Lamp
Copyright © 2011 Daniel Abdal-Hayy Moore
All rights reserved.
Printed in the United States of America


For quotes any longer than those for critical articles and reviews,
contact:
The Ecstatic Exchange,
6470 Morris Park Road, Philadelphia, PA 19151-2403
email: abdalhayy@danielmoorepoetry.com

First Edition
ISBN: 978-0-578-09592-9
Published by The Ecstatic Exchange,
6470 Morris Park Road, Philadelphia, PA 19151-2403

With thanks to my wife, Malika, and Tasneem Vandenberg, for
their helpful critiques.


Also available from The Ecstatic Exchange:
Knocking from Inside, poems by Tiel Aisha Ansari

Cover art and illustrations by the author
Back cover photograph by Malika Moore

بسم الله الرحمن الرحيم

# In the Name of Allah
# the Most Merciful the Most
# Compassionate

•

ENTER THIS TALE WITH OPEN HEART
AND FROM IT WITH WISE INSIGHT DEPART

THAT MORE IN THIS WORLD THAN WE CAN SEE
LEADS US TO GOD INVISIBLY

# INTRODUCTION (by the versifier)

Here's the classic tale of Ala-udeen (Arabic pronunciation, meaning *The Glory of the Way*) and the well-known genie (or jinn) in the magic lamp, with all its smoke-blasts of wondrous mystery, swift mind-boggling transformations, heartfelt love-longing for the princess of the sultan, innocent good versus evil (with good triumphant against black magicky dark forces), and in modern, narrative rhyming couplets for today's readers. Everyone's invited for this new version of the ancient Muslim wisdom story from *The Arabian Nights (Alf Layla wa Layla)*, or *A Thousand Nights and a Night*, so well-known as part of global consciousness that all you have to do is say "the magic lamp," and everyone knows what you're talking about, blue smoke-emerging genies and *"Your wish is my command!"* — but presented here in a sparkling new rendition.

If you're not familiar with the story, where anything can happen, and does, then you are in for a rare treat. But if you are, I invite you to my rhyming take on it, hitting all the main points, with a few improvisations of my own. I wrote it to read out loud before bedtime to kids ranging from about five to fifteen, while living in a Muslim community in Texas in the early 1980s. My *Abdallah Jones and the Disappearing-Dust Caper* came first, and this poem version not long afterwards. It's best read out loud, but read it without thinking of it as a poem at all, reading normally right through the lines, perhaps noticing some of the rhymes (sometimes comical), and "near rhymes" when words don't quite match up completely, such as, say, "cloud" and "would," or words that break at a syllable line-end and the next line-end word rhymes with it.

The story itself is full of profound echoes that remind us of such things as the great, powerfully mystical verse from the Holy Qur'an where a lamp is part of a complex metaphor for God (and though atoningly beautiful, not in any way the lamp of a jinn):

> *Allah is the Light of the heavens and the earth.*
> *The metaphor of His Light is that of a niche*
> *In which there is a lamp, the lamp inside a glass,*
> *the glass like a brilliant star, lit from a blessed tree, an olive,*
> *neither from the east nor of the west, its oil all but giving off light*
> *even if no fire touches it.* Light upon Light! (Qur'an: 24/35)

Our boy hero, poor Ala-udeen, falls in impossible love with the Sultan's daughter (before *Romeo and Juliet*, or Dante's love for Beatrice?), and this while in possession of a magic lamp whose obedient jinn is capable of bringing about a realization of his longing. It must be said also that for Muslims the normalcy of the jinn is a given, as God mentions their existence repeatedly in the Holy Qur'an, beings He created from smokeless fire (God created angels from light), with both good and evil temperaments, who coexist in an intersecting parallel universe with our own. So Ala-udeen's hankering can also be seen as our desire for nearness to Allah, the Divine Reality, Lord of all the Universes and Creator of ourselves and of our actions. But this world is an evanescent one, it comes and goes. Nothing is truly permanent in it, *including* ourselves. Palaces get built in a blink and disappear in a blink — which might be bewildering if we don't hold onto the rope of Allah throughout.

But the best echoes are those readers and listeners bring to bear to the story. May it entertain and bring joy as well as time-well-spent (even magical), and may it inspire greater creativity in our indigenous Way, with all my hope in God's continuous blessings on all of us, with always the happiest of outcomes, in this world and the next.

# CONTENTS

# Ala-udeen
## & The Magic Lamp

# CHAPTER 1: HOW HE GOT THE LAMP

Ala-udeen, as his name goes,
woke up with a bang and threw off his bedclothes,
rubbed his eyes, then jumped out of bed,
put his pants on, wound his turban on his head
and ran downstairs to the marketplace
having said his prayers and washed his face.

*China!* What a day! Sun high
in the egg-white China sky
and all the trees loaded with birds
who sang like little silver whistles. Absurd
to be gloomy on a day like this.

Ala-udeen knew it was a day that could not miss
being special. He ran to the fruit-stall
and when he saw the apples, he wanted them all
but he had only a few pennies.
He dug down into his pant's pockets, but couldn't find any
more money. So he walked up to the fruit-seller
and said: "I'll take that red one, and that bright yellow
apple, please, and here's my money.
*Bismillah!*" The seller was a grump. Nothing ever was funny.

He picked up the apples and plunked
them in a bag. Ala-udeen clunked

the pennies down on the table
and turned to go back to his house in the donkey-stable.

Meanwhile, a man with a strange straggly beard
across the market-square had been peering
through the crowd of people
watching Ala-udeen buy his morning apples.
Now he squinted his eyes and began to follow
Ala-udeen through the street as close as could allow
without being seen.

When the market ended, and the forest, green
and sunny began, the strange man
began to put into action his plan,
so he ran quietly through the trees to a bend in the road
and when Ala-udeen got there, strode
out into the sunlight and looked surprised.
His mouth dropped open. His two wily eyes
became round as saucers. He opened his arms
and cried out suddenly like someone alarmed,

"Is that you? Is it really you? Could it be?"
Ala-udeen replied, "Yes, it certainly is me!
Ala-udeen is my name. Is that good or bad?"
"Why, my boy, you look exactly like your dad!
You see, I'm his long lost most dearly beloved brother!"
"Well then, come on home, and you can talk to my mother."

The old man narrowed his eyes for a second,
then said, "Of course, let's go. What a godsend
to see you! You see, I've been far away

for about forty years, three and a half months and one day.
So if your mother doesn't recognize me, don't be surprised."

Ala-udeen was so happy he didn't notice the man's eyes
looking funny. But he did see the man's peculiar appearance.
Long black robe. Purple belt. Pointed shoes. A strange shuffling dance
as he walked by his side.

They got home to the humble house and went inside
and found Ala-udeen's old mother sitting by a hot pot of tea.
"Look mother! Here's my uncle who, by Allah, met me
coming out of the market, in the forest by the lake."
"Uncle?" his mother said. "Am I asleep, or awake?
I don't remember any uncle of yours that's still alive."

"Allow me to introduce myself, madam, I've
just come back after more than forty years away.
I don't think we've met. When my brother passed away,
your husband (fine man!), I was in far off Africa.
Or it may be I was selling polyester carpets in America…
I can't remember now. But I was definitely far away."

"But," she said, "if my husband had a brother, he didn't say."
"Well, early rivalry you know, young boys often fight.
I went off early, and dropped out of sight
to see the world and to seek my fortune.
Now, Ala-udeen, my nephew, soon
you will have some of it, for I have something special
to give you, but in secret, I can't tell
you here, if your mother will excuse us.
It's a very special gift, she cannot refuse us

permission to go out alone to a special place..."

He gave Ala-udeen's mother a wink with his crafty wrinkled face
leaning to one side.

So he and Ala-udeen went outside
and walked along the river to a place beyond the woods
between two mountains where they suddenly stopped, and stood
in one spot. At their feet were only leaves,
but the old man kicked them aside, leaving
a clear space in the dirt. "Now gather some sticks
and bring them here, we will fix
up a fire, and then you will see,"
and the old man chuckled to himself with a strange intensity.

When Ala-udeen came back, the man snatched
the sticks and threw them down, his patched
robe snagging on a twig, then started a fire
that grew so big he began to perspire,
then when it went up to the top of the sky
he suddenly threw in some red powders and let out a cry
in some mysterious language, pronouncing words
Ala-udeen had never ever heard
before, like "Ptax", or "Phitt", and strange
shadowy figures twisted in the fire, rearranging
blue smoke into faces and horses galloping into mist
while the twigs below sparkled, sighed and hissed.

Little Ala-udeen stood and watched, amazed,
when suddenly the fire stopped. Before him was raised
a square of earth, with a huge brass ring

sticking out of it. At this he started to sing
*"Help!"* and run away,
but the old man knocked him down, say-
ing, "I command you, the brother of your father, your uncle
to stay right here, or I'll give you a carbuncle
right on your skull! I mean, dear boy,
don't you see, this is no ordinary toy.
This is not just an afternoon's passing pleasure.
Down below this earth lies a marvelous treasure!"

With tears in his eyes, Ala-udeen said,
"Alright, I won't run away. I'll obey you instead."
So the old man changed like a whirlwind, and smiled
and embraced Ala-udeen, then in a voice sweet and mild
said: "Then grab that ring and pull, and you will see something that
    will amaze and astound you.

It will open up, and in the ground you
will see a stairway. Now you go right down
into the darkness, don't worry, around
ten steps down you will begin to see light,
not much, to be sure, but enough for your sight
to be clear. Now go straight ahead
to the bottom of the stairs. At the bottom is a door. Red
light will show it to you. You will open it.

Go into the palace, through three large halls, do not sit
in any of the golden chairs, don't touch the walls
even with your clothes, in fact don't touch anything at all
or you will die instantly. Do you understand?
Then when you come to the end, put out your hand

and open the door into the garden.

Go through it, and you will see planted all around in
it fruit trees, and wonderful flowers. But don't touch
anything, just go straight ahead, such
delights as you see will be everywhere,
so don't take anything at first. When you've breathed the air
which is like breezes of musk
go to the fountain in the middle, shining like polished elephant's
    tusk,
and right in the middle of the fountain there
is a niche, and you will see in it a marvelous lamp. Beware
of touching it too much. Take it and pour out the oil,
don't worry, it won't spoil
your clothes, for it is not really
what it seems, and the lamp will be
dry as soon as you tip it. So just pick it up
and come straight back, do you hear, don't stop
along the way, or loll around in the flowers,
it will only take a minute, although it may seem like hours,
but come straight back, and when you get to me
give me the lamp and then you will see
*miracles!*" So Ala-udeen grabbed the ring of brass

and the heavy earthen door in the grass
opened up and a stairway appeared. The old man then
slipped a small jade ring off his finger, and sent
Ala-udeen on his way putting it on one of his, saying: "This ring
    will guard you
against any evil. So long as you
obey me there is nothing to fear.

Do you hear
me?" Ala-udeen nodded, and so he

went down a step at a time, very slowly
since it was so dark. He looked back
at the man up above, in his black
robe, and his hands now rubbing together most strangely.

"He looks like he's rubbing his hands in glee,"
thought Ala-udeen. "Well, *bismillah*," he said,
as down he went, careful not to bump his head
on the opening, down and down he went
and at the tenth stair he saw red light, sent
by beams from he knew not where,
but it lit a little before him to the next stretch of stairs
down and down until he came to the door, it was open,
so he walked right in
to a magnificent palace, he knew
because latticework windows showed bright blue
sky outside, and on the wood-pieces crisscrossing
was carved the Name of Allah, so on everything
you saw through the windows you remembered
Who it was Who created it all, seen, tasted, or heard
in whatever world you happened to be in.

He went through the first hall, then through a thin
door, but he was careful not to touch it, then
he went through another hall, it seemed at least ten
times bigger than the first and took a long time to cross,
maybe an hour or so, but although the walls were like moss
and he really wanted to feel them

he kept his fingers to himself, as well as the hem
of his long shirt. His feet

whispered over the thick carpeting, sweet
incense filled the air he was in
until he came to a door even thin-
ner than the second one. He pulled himself tight
holding his breath, careful to step just right
through the third door.

Then he saw a clear glass floor
like a mirror stretch long across
an immense sumptuous hall all embossed
with gold leaves, and there were hundreds of gold
chairs along the walls, not new, not old,
but somehow timeless, even immaterial.
They sort of shimmered in the light, he wanted to touch the
    material
they were made out of, or sit down and rest.
But be remembered "instant death," so he did what was best
and moved on. The hall was full of
mirrors, and he saw himself multiplied, below and above,
since the floor and the ceiling
were also of crystal, until he felt he was reeling
like a drunken man, so much light and space,
and in each mirror the sight of the astonished small face
of Ala-udeen. Finally the hall passed out of sight
and he came out in a garden bathed in rainbow-colored light.

Giant peacocks made of crystalline feathers flew past,
and great trees of raspberries rose in a blast

of green light from the shores of a diamond-bright stream
that flowed past in curling ripples, each one a crescent-shaped beam
of light, dazzling little Ala-udeen's vision.
But he stood quite straight, and remembered his mission
which was to go straight on and not touch a thing.
To get to the fountain, find the lamp, then bring
it back up the stairway to where the old man stood.

He concentrated hard, and tried to still his blood
as it pumped quite excitedly through his heart.

One foot in front of the other, a sudden dart
of brilliance flashing past his face,
and the sky like blue opals filling all of space.

It was just too much for him. He almost sat down and waited.
He tried to walk a few steps, but he nearly fainted.
The smells alone were like perfumes he had never smelled.
When he got back home he would never be able to tell
what he found here
to his poor old mother.

But he said a loud "*Allahu akbar,*" and carried on,
went on walking with a very melodious song
on his lips of "*la ilaha illa Allah*" very clearly
and very strong. So that he very nearly
flew as he went walking along.

As things attracted his attention, he thought the old man might be
    wrong,
"There's no fountain here," he said to the air

as he walked past zebras, a giraffe and one blue polar bear
sitting with a lion licking his paws under a palm tree in the sun,
and snakes circling them by slithering in the grass as if run-
ning around them. He went on.

There was a trail of scallop shells through an emerald green lawn
that finally led to a fountain.
Water-spray spread great fans, high as a mountain
of drops, each one drumming,
and in the center in a niche of light, the lamp, shimmering, like a
    heartbeat thrumming.
The lamp, brass, with a handle, suspended in the spray.
"How can I possibly take it away?"

*"You will take me quite simply because of what is inside me."* Then it
    was silent.

So Ala-udeen stood on his toes, and bent
forward and reached in
and took hold of the lamp, neat as a pin,
and pulled it out of the fountain-spray
easy as pie, and took it away
to set it by him on the grass
as he sat down for a moment, to pass
a few minutes resting.

And all this time he didn't forget to sing
"*la ilaha illa Allah*," since that was his way
of concentrating on what he wanted, whatever distraction tried to play
tricks on him to make him totally forget
what it was in the first place he was told to get.

It was a simple lamp, antique, one of the pre-historic kind.
An oil-lamp. With a wick in it. Ones you don't find
these days. It had no electric cord attached,
no light-bulb or shade, but one you lit with a match,
and strangely, it was already burning,
even though it had been in the fountain, with water turning
all around it. A glow, a light, but with an oil that was like no oil
    inside it.
A gleam, very strong, that made fireflies flit
in circles and loops through its shedding glow.

Now he poured out the oil, and let it flow
onto the grass, but he was very surprised
because as soon as he poured it, what met his eyes
was nothing. Nothing at all. No
liquid, not a single thing that could show
it had been burning from some kind of fuel.
Then he took the wick, and it was dry, well-
twisted string of opposite strands
wound together in one unified band
that had been lit and cast light.

Ala-udeen now felt that everything was perfectly alright
forever. He had a lamp, and though
it was too early for him to know
what powers it had,
still it didn't seem bad
to him at all.
By Allah, it had fal-
len into his hands.
He might travel to far-off lands

and not find one like it again.
Then he thought of the old man.

"Better get going," he said to himself, and picked up
the lamp, and got up, and started to step
through the delicate grass-blades of the cool
garden, past monkeys playing in a pool
of pink water, past beavers and sea
otter, water-snakes and gold-fish in pea-
green shadows under ledges
of moss. The path wound around hedges
of golden droplets hanging lightly
as bells that tinkled slightly
as he walked past. He went faster
and faster, not touching anything, past
fruit trees like he'd never ever seen before
and then he just had to stop, before he got to the door
and just take a closer look. He was in a kind of orchard
of fruit trees quite symmetrically placed. He overheard
a whisper of birds' voices high
in far off clouds of glistening sky
say, in the voice of the magician,
*"Take as many fruits here as you possibly can.*
*It will do you no harm now."*

At first he wasn't too sure, how
would he get them all home? Then
he remembered his big pockets, sewn in the hem
of his shirt, so be began to wander
through the orchard, and slowly meander
under the trees lush with fruit.

They were the most beautiful loot
he had ever seen. Emeralds, green, bright diamond
pineapples hanging, dazzling like the sun
in supernatural light, pearl clusters of grapes and turquoises,
berries so blue, and all making noises
like small bells or voices as they
tinkled together in breezes that say,
*"We come from Allah, and to Allah we return."*
Desire for some of them began to burn
in his heart, so with the lamp inside his shirt tucked
in his belt he stood up on tip-toe and sucked
in his breath
as he braved instant death
by plucking them slowly, the stems gently snapping.
He was grateful to see that nothing bad was happening.

Soon his pockets were full, in fact they were bulging,
since as soon as one was plucked, he began to indulge
himself, until he was quite laden down.
He was up in a tree. Now he jumped to the ground
and walked on as before
until he got to a door,
which he opened
and found
himself standing at the top of the topmost stair
in the forest, where the old man stood, his stare
boring into Ala-udeen's two eyes like a pair of corkscrews.

*"Aha!* Give me the lamp, boy, don't you
hold onto it now. That's it, *come on!"*
But Ala-udeen just stood there, his arm pressed upon

the lamp, and the pockets of his shirt so hugely stuffed
that the opening in the earth just wasn't wide enough
for him to squeeze through now.
"Please sir," he called out, "how
can I get out?" "Don't play games with me, son,
hand me that lamp, I'm the one
in charge here!" But Ala-udeen was stuck
and couldn't reach to where it was tucked
into his shirt, so he said, "Help me out first!"

But at that moment the man suddenly burst
into a fury. Tore his hair. Scratched his face in a rage.
Ala-udeen just stood there, patient as a sage
sitting on a cushion at night.
But the old man was a terrible sight.
Blood pouring out of his eyes. Great fangs
from his mouth. Long yellow fingers, jangling
bells as he jumped up and down on the grass.

*"You hand over that lamp, or I will make you pass
into the next world like a smoke puff."*
The old man was getting pretty rough
now, he stomped on the ground, and yelled some
incantations the boy didn't understand, but something awful was
    about to come,
he could tell, they were deadly serious.
The old man turned nearly yellow, he was so fanatically furious.

Ala-udeen said, *"Allah!"* He knew it was his protection.
Little did he know the old man was crazy. He saw he couldn't be
    his uncle. He had not allowed much inspection

into his past.
He was chanting faster and fast-
er now and twirling higher than his length,
then all of a sudden, as if from magic strength,
the earth that had covered the entrance to the stairway
slammed shut, trapping Ala-udeen inside with no way
out. With a long last shout, the old man flew far off
back to Africa with a snort and an angry scoff.

This was no uncle. This nasty old magician
had found out about the lamp from a fiendish mathematician
and decided he had to get it
but needed someone who could easily fit
through first the earth-door, then the last thin door,
and that is how Ala-udeen, a long time before
they met had been so specially chosen,
for Destiny, by Allah, is anything but frozen.
It was all by Allah that he was so conveniently small and thin.

He started to cry out impatiently, since he found himself locked in,
*"O here's your lamp, please take it!"*

But at last had to sit
on the top stair in the dark
and consult his own heart.

# CHAPTER 2: THE RING, THE LAMP, AND THE JINN

"Oh Allah! what shall I do? Here I am trapped!"
But Ala-udeen was not afraid! since his *iman* had not snapped
face to face with danger, or even death. He knew Allah was near,
so it was a slight claustrophobia he felt, not really fear,
since it was so dark and wet, and the stairway went straight down.
This is what was in his heart as he sat underground.

Finally he felt his way along, down and down each cautious stair
until he got down to the door and found it shut, so now there
was nowhere to go. He said, in his heart concentrating in this dark
    with no light-beam:
*"La howla wa la quwata ila billahi 'ali al-Atheem,"*
*"No power, no strength, but from Allah, the High, the Great."*
And then he thought that he would simply do the prayer and wait
for death. Just like that. After all, if he was really already inside the
    earth,
then this might just as well be the destined end of his life that was cast
    before his birth.

He was still in *wudhu* from morning. He found a place to stand,
and before he did the first *"Allahu akbar"* he happened to rub one hand
against the other, and in so doing
he happened to rub that ring
the magician had given him.

Suddenly the air grew full as if it were filled to its very brim,
and there was a tremendous crack of thunder, its catastrophic sound
trembling all the earth, above, below, three-dimensionally around
him. The walls shook, the floor shook, everything was shaking.
Only Ala-udeen was saved from the generalized quaking
for the Divine Name was booming in his heart and silently on his lips.
So he just stood there as tall and still as he could as light flashed and
    dust slipped
and shivered all around him,
when suddenly a bright light shot up in the dim
cavern, and there standing before him in billows of yellow smoke
was a giant jinn in a green turban big as a house who now thunderously
    spoke:

> *"Your wish is my command,*
> *in whoever's hand*
> *the ring may be on,*
> *for I and the other jinn*
> *are only slaves, and we obey.*
> *So, master, ask without delay!"*

Little Ala ud-Deen, a tiny ant in the jinn's looming shadow,
looked up in astonishment at the massive furrowed brow
and crossed arms of this giant, and fearlessly replied:
"Take me out of here, please, *Oh please*, take me outside!"

So in a flash the jinn transported him, lamp and ring and all,
the jeweled fruit still stuffed as you would stuff a huge ball
into each pocket. He now found himself on top
in the grassy place where he started with that old mop-
head of a magician, but now no door,

no brass ring, no square of earth as before
even showed where it had been.

Ala-udeen was astonished, for there was no trace of jinn
either. Nothing to show it had ever even happened.
Except he *did* have the booty, the jeweled fruit, and the lamp that
    nearly brought a bad end
to it all. Allah had brought him out of the dark into the light.
*"Alhamdulillah!"* he said, shaking himself, "it turned out alright!"

He dusted off his clothes and did two *rakats* of thanks,
then gathered his lamp and his fruits, since all the recent magical pranks
of the afternoon seemed over, and none too soon.
He went home along the forest trail by the light of the full moon.

When he got home he was hungry, for he had not had anything to eat,
and exhausted more than he knew, in fact he was dead on his feet.
So when the door opened, he collapsed. His mother carried him in.
And when he woke up many hours later, he pointed to his thin
belly where his little ribs showed their shape
and said, "Dear mother, is there a piece of bread in the house, or even
    a solitary grape?"

"No, my boy, there is nothing, the whole house is absolutely empty.
But what happened to you? I even thought you had taken ship and
    gone to sea!"
So he told everything that had happened, about the lamp and
    the magician.
"I was always a little suspicious about that sulfurous-smelling man!"
He showed her the lamp, and the extraordinary fruit.
She was startled by the jeweled brilliance, she became totally mute

when she saw it. But the lamp impressed her less.

It was a bit battered in the daylight, and looked like it was only made of
   brass

or copper. "But mother, if it's food we need, I will take the lamp to the
   market,

and with the money I sell it for then I can surely get

all the food we need for breakfast, maybe even lunch and dinner!"

"Well, perhaps" she said, "but it's really quite dirty. You might sell it if it
   were cleaner."


So she took a corner of her apron and began to give it a rub

when, with a volcanic crack of thunder, and a celestial hubbub

the form of a jinn billowed up from the spout of the lamp and went
   right through the ceiling,

but there was no sound of cracking, or rafters breaking, or paint
   peeling,

as sparks of yellow and blue flamelets outlined his incredible bulk

as it shot up in another dimension beyond the realm of the *mulk*

without disturbing the plates on the shelf or the cobwebs in the corners.


His belt flashed gold, his scimitar blade probably made many men
   mourners.

His face and figure were terrible, wreathed with silver smoke hot and
   sooty,

but although he loomed fiercely above them, he had a strange kind of
   beauty.

His skin was a color unlike anything, his shirt was a fine brocade,

ruby and turquoise threads blinking like lights at a penny arcade.


This all happened faster than atoms in a reactor,

and his mother reacted rather badly, since it rather shocked her,

and when he had telescoped up full height it was a twelve-story jinn
    that appeared.
She fainted dead away. She had never seen anything so weird.

But Ala-udeen wasn't surprised, he caught the lamp before it fell,
and sat still as a rock before that apparition as it began to tell
its rhyme:

> *"Your wish is my command*
> *in whoever's hand*
> *the lamp may be in,*
> *for I and the other jinn*
> *are only slaves, and we obey.*
> *So, master, ask without delay!"*

"Please, O jinn of this lamp, me and my mother are terribly hungry.
Could you bring us some food, with perhaps a slice of *halal* turkey?"
And before a moment had passed, or even a fraction of a fraction,
a whole twelve-course feast was laid out, by means of invisible action.
Trays of polished silver, each one tooled more complex than the next.
Covered dishes and huge serving bowls, and a complicated nest
of trays, one inside the other, all with delicious-smelling meats
cooked in exaggerated sauces, with fruits both sour and sweet,
and almonds dripping butter, and more turkey than you could count,
all displayed on a lacy tablecloth, and in the center an artificial fount-
ain of purest milk with droplets of purest honey.
This was a far more extravagant feast than you could possibly buy with
    money.

Ala-udeen's eyes widened. But he was not overwhelmed.
"*Allahu akbar!*" he said out loud, "this is all from the purest realm

of the *malakut.* Just look at it! Such silver eyes have never seen.
It gleams and glistens like starlight with its superstellar sheen!"
He sprinkled water on his mother's face, and she sat up with a start.

"What was that apparition? I thought I suffered an attack of my heart!"
"Come, mother, let's eat now. Look, this food is here, hot, waiting!"
"How did it get here, my son? Did the sultan pay his *zakat* or
	something?"
"It doesn't matter, it's not important. It all happened while you napped.
It's from Allah, that's for sure, a little bit of His abundant bounty just
	snapped
off the tree and landed on our table — *Yes, that's it!*
Now come on mother, it's getting cold, just sit
and have some glacéd quince, or roasted pigeon, or that juice with the
	brewer's yeast."

And so Ala-udeen and his mother passed the whole morning savoring a
	feast
such as they had never had in all their lives, it was so absolutely
	sumptuous.

"Now tell me everything, Ala-udeen, if I'm not being too
	presumptuous."
So he told her of the jinn of the lamp, and the jinn of the magic ring.
"But jinn are made of smokeless fire, not light. I'll not have anything
to do with them! I want to be in the highest company of the angels.
The Prophet, *salallahu alayhi wa salam,* told us all about the jinn, and we
	don't pour boiling water down wells
or throw rocks at cats, for fear of angering those unangelic creatures.
Please, Ala-udeen, throw the lamp and ring away. Why, when I
	simply remember the grisly features

of that jinn again, I almost faint — it's not just idle play!"

"But mother, the lamp must be worth really something for that magician
    to have come all the way
from Africa to China to get it."
His mother simply said, *"Forget it!"*

But Ala-udeen finally obtained his scrupulous mother's permission
to keep both ring and lamp, to be used only with the utmost discretion.
So they lived for years, in the same humble house, and, by Allah,
    occasionally feasted,
and then by selling the silver trays brought by the jinn, they comfortably
    subsisted
from day to day, but simply, not living in the lap of luxury.
"Abundance only comes from Allah," he would say, "though the fruit
    comes from the tree."

Years passed. No one knew that the boy and his mother were wealthy.
They lived for years as they had always lived. Their eyes clear, their cheeks
    healthy
with robustness. They were generous. They gave gifts to their neighbors
    each day.

And so time passed, though they lacked nothing, in the most usual way.
Ala-udeen was growing up now, he learned the ways of the world.
He talked to merchants and walked in the streets with lips curled
in a graceful smile. He had even learned during this time
that the fruits he gathered in that garden down below were the finest
    jewels of their kind
though he showed them to no one.

So, upon a handsome youth now the full rays of the late-morning sun
fell in their seasonal slant.
He was flowering in his fullness now, like a sturdy desert plant.

Then one day, one momentous day, as he passed in the usual street,
he heard a crier running along, over and over made to repeat
the same thing: "Everyone is ordered to stay indoors all morning until
    noon,
for the sultan's daughter, Princess Badroulbadour (meaning *"full moon of
    full moons"* ) soon
will be passing this way as she goes from the palace to take her Friday
    bath,
and the sultan orders that no one see her, and that all be cleared from
    her path!"

Now Ala-udeen, although grown up, was still a bit of a rascal,
and he conceived in his heart the desire to glance at this damsel as she
    went to her task, all
protected and covered and veiled and surrounded by her twenty
    ladies-in-waiting,
so he hid by the bath behind a door so he could peek at her through
    a grating.
She lived such a life of seclusion, no one outside the palace could ever be
    allowed to see her, from far away or close up,
which only increased his eager hope to get a clear glimpse of her before
    the bath house doors could close up.

Then she passed. He was overwhelmed. Nothing he had ever seen before,
neither garden, jewels, silver nor jinn had beauty that could knock him
    to the floor,
his knees buckling.

She was an extraterrestrial thing.
She had a purely celestial delicacy.
Her face, unveiled by any cloth, showed especially
a silver-like purity and fineness.
She had eyebrows that arched high, less
like hairs than like archers' bows,
and her moon-like face had an exquisitely shaped nose
and small ruby-red lips, dark eyes, large lids,
her high cheekbones so chiseled, it rids
one of the power to describe her.
You would have to imbibe her.
Drink her beauty. For it was Allah's beauty, in all its manifest Light.

He caught a fleeting glimpse of it. Then she passed out of sight
into the bath-house, the doors slamming. He stood for a long time
    transfixed.
He could not move. The thoughts in his mind and the movements in his
    heart mixed
like two entwining vapors.
He could only remember those deep dark eyes that had lights like
    glowing tapers.
Her fragrance remained. He shook himself. He looked at his hands and
    his clothes.
*"I must marry that Princess,"* he said, *"as sure as my own blood flows!"*

So he slid from the door and ran to his house and sat in his room alone.
For days he sat sunk deep in thought, wouldn't eat, not even a bone
could tempt his appetite, he was so completely absorbed. He grew pale.
He trembled at a melodious voice, or a smell from some flower as its
    scent faintly sailed
across the room past his nostrils. He sat still.

He was as one dead. He was lovesick. He was ill
though he was really well.
It was Allah's way to wake him up and make him take the journey from
the magic spell
of human sleep to the more-than-human Path that leads to Him.
For that one glimpse of beauty beyond the norm had filled his heart
to the brim.

Finally he appeared at the door of his room and said to his variously
worried mother,
*"I must marry the daughter of the sultan! I will never marry any other!"*
His mother just laughed. She couldn't believe it. So that was what was
wrong!
"How can you possibly do that, my boy, not even if you write her a song
the angels could sing to her could you hope to win her from the confines
of her life in the palace.
Look, she is surrounded by servants and guards and wise men, she has
goblets and a diamond chalice
she drinks her orange juice from. Ala-udeen, my son, wake up my
boy, how could you?"

"You will go to the sultan and ask her hand in marriage to me, you will do
it tomorrow. Please, don't worry, you will take a gift the sultan cannot
refuse.
The fruits I brought back from that garden, in a basket, wrapped in fine
tissues!"

So they placed the gems, the bright green emeralds and the grapes of
glittering pearls,
in a basket made of spun silver strands woven and ending in curls
of silver threads. The fruits lay in that bed and like astonishing starlight

glittered.

An expression full of hope and bright inner sight across Ala-udeen's
gaunt face flittered

as his mother went out the door next day, basket over her arm, to the
sultan.

He stood in the door and watched her go. For he was now becoming a
man.

# CHAPTER 3: THE MIRAGE AND THE MARRIAGE

The sultan was kind, he was generous and crafty,
he always wore splendid robes in halls both vast and drafty
as he sat high on his elevated throne above the people who came to
see him
so he could look down on them from an imposing height,
reminding everyone that they could not *be* him.

He didn't read the Qur'an unless it was embossed in gold,
but he always kept one next to him in a wooden chest, old
hinges and locks and jewels set in patterns around it,
and his highly paid scholars who, when asked for a judgment
always found it
either in Qur'an from an ambiguous sign
or a *hadith* whose chain might not be so fine,
or even doubtful.

The sultan's vanity was true, a real snoutful
of self-importance that allowed him to falsify Allah's Truth while
everyone agreed.
They would shuffle up to him in his audience chamber in their
hour of need.
He would lean forward, listen a little, read little notes on paper,
consult with his *wazir,* also dressed in gold, who sat with his gold
telephone and newspaper

watching the stock market, getting calls from Aramco and other
   American oil companies
while Ala-udeen's mother came and sat in the back with the basket
   on her knees.


For the sultan and his people had left the pure pattern of Madina
at the time of the Prophet, peace be upon him, and so they didn't
   lean on a
firm support when making their judgments or final decisions,
but changed things, added things, or cut things out with some
   deep incisions
and the pure balance of the *Deen of Allah* was lost.
The heart of Islam, for them, became covered with frost.
Their social *qibla* was riches. Power. Expansion. High Living.
Although they prayed and fasted, and were not against often giving
great sums of money to someone in need.
It's just that the basic passion that ruled them was simple greed.
It made the sultan a weak man. He didn't reflect from pure source.
He was emotional, whimsical, which is not true Islam, and could
   often force
someone to do things with threats, or torture, or even death.
He perfumed himself. He lavished rose water on himself. He even
   perfumed his breath
with mints as he sat in fantasy splendor under gold chandeliers,
while his cynical *wazir* and counselors concealed disdainful sneers.
It was far off the mark.
Like someone who's given up the Path to set off in the dark.


So Ala-udeen's mother sat patiently to one side, basket on her knee,
as the sultan heard case after case, theatrically
leaning to hear an old shepherd croak out

a request, or shed a tear, or an angry merchant shout
some obscene injustice. But then the sultan got up and left.

The day was over. She was abandoned, bereft,
with the brimful basket on her knee
and her son's request unheard. Patiently
she returned next morning. She sat in the same spot.
Each day the sultan noticed her, but as the jabbering and complaints
    grew hot
he would forget her. But one day he leaned over to the *wazir* to say:
    "Call that woman over if she comes again.
She always sits in the same place behind the men.
She keeps her eyes down. But I can tell
she's got something important. As well,
there's that covered silver basket on her knee
*I'm really dying to see!*"

So on the sixth day one of the court men in his robes
came and got her. She was flushed and excited to the lobes
of her ears. She bowed before the sultan
as she would before the most important of men.
Then she said, when asked her request,
"Please forgive me and pardon me beforehand, I'd feel best
if you did so now."
The sultan raised one eyebrow
and waved his hand in answer.
The old woman trembled. "Well, you see, sir,
it's my son. He saw your daughter that day
as she went to the bath, on her way
through the door, and he told me,
he said: 'When she went into the dark, she

was like the full moon at its fullest in the pitch black blackest sky!'
He's not been able to get her beauty out of the innermost eye
of his heart. He is like a desperate, shipwrecked, heartbroken
man. But something in him has woken
up bigger than you or me.
Allah knows our destiny.
So, sir, I have come to ask for her hand in marriage to my son.
I fear if he cannot marry her, he will not marry anyone."

"And what is this," the sultan asked, leaning forward, "there by
    your knee?
Is it something you have brought here to the palace for me to see?"
She uncovered the silver basket.
The sultan's eyes grew fantastic-
ally wide, and so did the *wazir's,*
and everyone at his side, to see the scissors
of light snip through the air coming from those sparkling jewels.
Everyone in the *diwan* crowded around, their faces as thunderstruck
    as fools'
faces before that bubbling splendor.
They'd never seen anything ever before
to match them. The sultan cleared his throat.

"Ah-hem, madam! These fruits with their dazzling light make my
    eyes float
in a space that is truly spectacular.
Why I'm nearly speechless. There just aren't the right words to describe
    them in our modern vernacular!"

He turned to his *wazir* whose face was flushed
with red as if he'd just grown angry or blushed,

and the sultan said, "Certainly, this is grand!
Why should I not give my daughter, the Princess' hand
to someone who values her as highly as this?
This is a prize, by Allah, she should not miss!"

But the *wazir*'s face now grew stormy gray
like clouds when they gather on a soot-black day
before a rainstorm.
He'd had a brainstorm.
"If you wait three months, O great sultan of the faithful,
for *my* son, an approved-of suitor for your daughter, I'd be grateful,
for that would give him time
to come up with a dowry at least as fine
as these paltry baubles."
(His son was something of a lout, shiftless and lazy, and even unkempt,
taking full advantage of his status as "entitled," thinking himself exempt
from good manners or courtesy, or even being smart.
Alas for the Princess to be married to him, with her pure and sensitive
    heart.)

But the sultan threw back his shoulders, like one throwing off troubles,
and said: "Alright, I'll grant the marriage to your son, good woman,
    but in the space of three months from now.
Go home, and tell your son to wait ninety days for the marriage vow."
She bowed low, leaving the jewels, and left the room.
She rushed home. Her old voice boomed
triumphantly to her impatient son, whose face
burst into smiles and light shone from the space
of his eyes and his brow
as it had not done until now.

They lived as they had, two months dragged on.

Then one night, when the oil ran out, she left her son
to go out to the market to the open stall
of the oil-seller. But the city was decked out for a festival,
bright yellow lights shone above the streets,
balloons and streamers and fireworks repeating
splatters of gold and rose sparks in the sky
high up above their heads. She had to cry
out loudly above the cheering and the shouts
to find out what the celebration was all about.

"The *wazir's* son," the oil-seller said,
then they were interrupted, she got knocked on the head,
then after apologies, she pushed her way back, cupping her ear
 so she'd be able to hear
as he went on, "I said, the *wazir's* son
is getting," then there was someone
who shouted so loud she could hear nothing. Then bubbling
     laughter. The pitch of the noise grew tauter.
"I said, tonight the *wazir's* son is marrying... *the sultan's daughter!*"

Everything went silent. Ala-udeen's mother went numb.
For an endless minute she was like someone struck dumb.
She grew dizzy. Then when she had steadied herself, she turned
     from the oil-seller and fled.
She ran into the house and shook Ala-udeen awake from his bed.
"Tonight," she blustered, "it's too late, the sultan lied!"
He could hardly understand a word she said as she broke down
     and cried.
Finally he got it straight. He just smiled,

and left her alone in her sympathetic grief for a little while
to go consult his lamp. "*Hasboon Allahu wa neamal wakeel.*
*Allah is enough for me, and the best guardian,*" and he began to feel
for the special place.
He rubbed. The jinn thundered his twelve-story high appearance
  in space
and bowed low in the strange mist swirling beyond sense-perception
  that always came with him.
Only his voice was not dim:

> *"Your wish is my command*
> *in whoever's hand*
> *the lamp may be in,*
> *for I, and the other jinn,*
> *are only slaves, and we obey.*
> *So master, ask without delay!"*

"Well, jinn, this is the proposition.
It's a strange situation we find ourselves in."
(His mind, cool but now whirring, thought of the Princess marrying
  that arrogant fool, who looked down on everyone
elder with long gray beard, scholar or brilliant ingenious son,
and he was well-known for his wayward way with women,
dallying with this one and that one in the court, breaking hearts with
  his Casanova-like venom.)
Ala-udeen continued: "I hope I'm not asking too much.
You've always served us with such
fine manners, and so obediently.
All those dishes and trays piled up so lusciously
with food. But now it's something more difficult.
I pray to Allah for a good result.

The sultan's daughter is being married tonight
to the *wazir's* son, and I want you to transport them right
here just at the moment the festivities have begun to thin
and the two newlyweds excuse themselves to go in
to the bed-chamber.
Now, can you remember?"
The jinn bowed low and disappeared.
Ala-udeen went and told his mother there was nothing to be feared
tonight.
It would all turn out right,
*insha'Allah.* So they had their supper
in their simple house in the donkey-stable, the upper
floor above the strong, ripe, natural smells,
...while at the palace, the feast filled the halls with crystal bells
and gongs and trumpets, the singing and dancing
that heats up the blood and makes the bride to the bridegroom
        so enticing, so entrancing.

And when the night wore on, the couple fled,
for now it was time for them to go to bed.
But as soon as they sat on it, suddenly
they were lifted into the air by that swift jinn, he
swooped faster than light to Ala-udeen's room
where he told the jinn to please remove the bridegroom
and keep him prisoner outside until dawn.
He was taken away without a moan
for the jinn had blown a breath of air on him
that put him in a trance that completely transfixed him,
so he stood like a statue outside Ala-udeen's door
in the freezing cold and smelly corridor.
(But let's not sympathize — he was a frightful bore.)

Then Ala-udeen turned to the Princess.
"Please, Princess, forgive me for this,
but this moment could not be delayed.
Your father, the sultan, betrayed
me. I asked for your hand in marriage, and he gave me three
     months!"
Then Ala-udeen told her everything, how once
he saw her he had to marry her, and when he knew they'd be married,
     he'd patiently waited
until it should happen as it was fated.
Shy as she was, she was also deeply relieved.
The vizier's son was more boorish than could be believed,
plus Ala-udeen obviously loved her to go to such length,
which increased him in her eyes who admired such strength.
She saw into his heart, and knew it was pure.
She said, "You're so brave to save me, though I'm not quite sure
how you did it!"
But Ala-udeen's happy face slid it
out of her mind, so she trusted Allah completely.
She saw in his eyes the depth of his sincerity, bubbling sweetly.

They sat apart and shy like two innocent creatures,
the moonlight through the window bathing her delicate features
and Ala-udeen amazed. Soon they'd be married, if Allah willed.
He let her doze, and watched her from afar, heart stilled
and calm. In the morning he had the jinn fly her all the way
home, after getting her chilly husband out from the cold hallway
frozen to the bone. They were flown, bed and all, back to their bedroom,
where the sultan was coming to greet the bride and the lucky
     bridegroom.

The man was a pale blue color.
He could hardly speak. He'd stood all night out in the corridor.
He fled to the closet
when the sultan came in to visit
his daughter, but found her seemingly melancholy.
"Why is this, my dear daughter, I thought you'd be jolly!"
But she kept silent.

So off he went, and then he sent
her mother to her, where she immediately
flew into her arms and cried out in well-simulated misery
the whole strange tale of the wedding night.
"Sh-sh-sh, daughter, don't speak of it to anyone, people will think
    you are not quite right
in the head."
So the story was kept secret instead.
The next day, rejoicing,
all the townspeople voicing
the joy of the marriage,
but when night came, the aerial bed-carriage
again carried them off through the sky
with sheets and canopy fly-
ing, the great jinn underneath,
groom without sword or sheath,
to Ala-udeen's bedroom
where again he removed the sweet bride from the bridegroom
and made him stand hypnotized
in the hallway surprised
by a deep frozen trance,
the great romance-
buster.

He could never muster
enough strength to win.

So when the jinn
flew them back to the palace in the morning again
finally the Princess told all to her father, the sultan,
about the fantastic flight
in the dead of night
by an unknown force,
beyond this world, of course,
without mentioning Ala-udeen.

So in the *majlis* that day the sultan stood up, and the sun shone in
    the sheen
of his glittering eyes as he declared in his voice
of authority the dissolving of the marriage, by choice
of destiny. Allah had definitely not wanted it.
The *wazir's* son was certainly not fit
to be his son-in-law!
It was totally forgotten. No one ever saw
the *wazir's* son again.
That's how it is for some sad men.
A bad apple in every bunch.

Then when three months finally passed, over lunch,
Ala-udeen mentioned to his mother the date
and sent her off, smiling to himself, so she would not be late
for the sultan's consultation. She arrived and took her place
and when the sultan saw her face
again he was startled, having so totally forgotten
the three-month old proposition.

She bowed low again as previously,
then lifted her head up undeviously
genuinely hopeful, and said, "O sultan, those three long months
    are up
and my son impatiently waits to sup
with your daughter in their wedding chamber,
in a privacy of doves, the amber
light of morning playing on her moonlike face."
The sultan shifted uneasily in his place
and said, "Well, we shall see.
If he is able to have brought to me
forty golden trays, each one gluttonously full
of jeweled fruit, more splendid than those first ones that pulled
my attention toward you, piled to the ceiling carried by servants
each upright one of them one of God's viceregents,
pure-hearted, bright-eyed,
totally believing true-blood, dignified
servants! *A procession of sanctity!*
Then, and only then, we shall see
if my daughter would truly be well taken care of
if entrusted to your son's love."

So the mother trudged home again,
downhearted after seeing the sultan
not hopeful her son could come up with such treasure.
But Ala-udeen only smiled with secret pleasure
and went to his room. He rubbed the lamp. The jinn appeared.
He outdid the request, and though Ala-udeen feared
it would not be sumptuous enough,
what the jinn assembled was extraordinary stuff.

Silver and gold oddments, trinkets that jingled
wrapped in costly cloths with vermillion and gold threads
    intermingled
in zigzag patterns that curled around embroidered berry-vines
    and tulips,
and opal-studded sherbet-shaped icy-edged juleps
in round dangling flounces, and melons and kiwi
sliced emeralds that glittered in millions of pee-wee
tiny facets. It was much too extravagant.
But the servants stood in rows outside Ala-udeen's apartment
shouldering these trays.
(You don't often see sights like this these days!)
At a signal they set off, and they were greeted by crowds
of people on the sidewalks, astonished as this treasure plowed
its way to the palace, before the sultan retired
from his audience for the day. The richness fired
the people's hearts with its array of visual wonder.
Such other-worldly plunder!
The sultan allowed the parade to enter,
and its crystalline procession filed to the very center
of the palatial throne-room,
lights radiating out in a zoom
lens of magnified glittering.
So much light filled the room, the children couldn't help tittering.
But the sultan was impressed.

"O Princess," he said, "get dressed
for your wedding! O woman, go tell your son
I await him here with open arms, the setting sun
in all its royal radiance has not shed her beams
on someone as happy as I, nor could dreams

of perfect extraterrestrial Utopias
match, with overflowing cornucopias,
my joy.
*Go get that boy!"*
So Ala-udeen's mother bowed again, and again
ran home, this time with the good news that the sultan
was waiting for him, to receive him as his own son.
He lowered his eyes. His heart was turning like a pin-wheel spun
by a summer breeze. He excused himself.
Went into his room. Said, *"Al-hamdulillah wa shukrulillah,"* was
    beside himself
with joy. He finally could only say: *"Allah!"* Loud.
A long, low sound, that resounded abroad
through those stables,
shaking the tables.

Then he took the lamp down from the shelf.
He rubbed it, and when the jinn showed himself
towering in that tiny room, through another dimension,
Ala-udeen said to him, "O jinn of the lamp, with no hesitation,
speed me to the *hammam*, I want a good scrub,
fine oils, good scents, aloes, musk, a hot tub
attended by invisible attendants.
I want to be as if alone. Then when I'm covered in fine scents,
please, a robe whose visual magnificence
outdoes anything the sultan has, no chintz
or simple muslin,
but cloth fit for a Muslim!"
In a flash he was there.
Undressed, but unaware
by whom, in the tall steamy hall of the bath,

hot, one room hotter than the last, a gray mist shot through with
     math-
ematical precision by dot-beams of sunlight,
and the heat just right
to make him perspire all the unnatural toxins out
as he lay like one dead. He was given a clout
here and a pummel there by an expert masseur,
although he couldn't see him, no one to say, "Yes, sir,"
to him. And as he lay there and the beads of sweat
came off his brow like a hot cascade, he began to get
visions of the Fire, fearful, the awful eternity of it, the torture,
     the steam,
billows of sulfurous heat worse than a bad dream.
He felt his heart throbbing with its bodily pressure
intensified, then slowly released, light like a treasure
from the ocean-floor inside him gradually shooting its gold beam
upward through his hot blood to wake him up from the bad dream
at last. Then he was turned over and over like a corpse in the hands
     of a washer,
and then given a good slosh
all over by buckets of cooler water.
He was slowly being purified and transformed to marry the sultan's
     daughter!

Later he lay on a bed with a wool blanket
sipping green tea from a straw, and a distant door clanked
shut as the invisible attendants departed.
Ala-udeen lay still and drowsing, clean and light-hearted.
In the room where he left his clothes,
he was amazed to see trousers and shirt and robe unlike those
made by swiftest human hands with quick silver needle

working eternities of late hours, tailoring to feed
little mouths. No human labor however extra-special
could have made such overwhelmingly supernatural
cloth. Even though he squinted, he could not see threads, nor
    weave, nor any handiwork,
but depths of rainbow-colored pattern in otherworldly artwork
showed scenes of rivers and waterfalls from cliffs,
with clouds in moonlight, and drifts
of mist and light
that dazzled his eye, it was so bright.
He put them on. His skin was different.
His hands were smooth. He became aware that his skin and
    eyes and hair were all lent
by Allah for this world's fast moment, spent,
and then, the senses returned to their source, sent
on. He adjusted his clothes, and went
on. Outside, the jinn had graciously supplied him with all
    his wants,
a horse that surpassed all the sultan's in its sleek magnificence,
handsome as a mountain, tall as a forest,
fleet as currents of the swiftest
river, white as icebergs, alert as snow.
And behind it, arranged in seemingly infinite rows,
servants with platters heaped with mounds of gold coins
with instructions for them to toss them to the crowds that would
    soon join
the procession. And servants with similarly tailored clothes
for his mother, to be finer than any of those
worn by the sultan's four wives.
They would see the sight of their lives
when they saw her.

He then set out to see his new father-
in law.
It was the most magnificent procession you ever saw.
Coins like fountains sprayed up in the air
and the crowds of people that gathered everywhere
were jubilant, praising Allah, glad
that in their realm it would soon be 'Ala ud-
deen that would marry the Princess.
They had seen no one as
generous as he. He arrived at the door of the palace.
He was ushered in. He went to the throne. He bowed low and
    showed a face
of modesty, noble. He was dignified,
the sultan was deeply gratified
and had him sit next to him.
He called the *cadi* in,
the marriage contract was drawn up
and the bride's consent was sup-
plied with a bowed head and a smile
and then she and her ladies filed
out for their own wedding party as Ala-udeen and the sultan
watched acrobats and the court musician
play music that interlinked the most distant heavens.
The sultan then turned to Ala-udeen, and in an even
voice, asked him, "Will you conclude the marriage tonight
here in the palace?" "No, sir. First I must build a palace of my own
    right
nearby. Please, I would like a bit of land to build
a palace where the Princess's heart may become still
and tranquil."

The sultan rose and strode across the room to the window-sill
and pointed out across the garden to a large round hill
and said, "That is yours!"
Ala-udeen replied, "If Allah wills, it will be built before
tomorrow at sunrise."

He bowed and left the sultan and all his men with their tea-glasses
    suspended in midair in astonished surprise.

# CHAPTER 4: THE PALACE OF LIGHT AND THE DARK CLOUD

When Ala-udeen was again alone in his room
in the creaky shadows above the donkey stable, he soon
took the lamp and again summoned
the jinn to come and produce wonders from the inexhaustible fund
of Allah's abundance.

"O jinn, please, once
I asked you for trays of food, then jewels, and the finest thoroughbred.
Now I command you to build the finest palace this borough has ever
     had.
A great hall with exquisite turquoise and shell mosaics,
star patterns repeated from floor to ceiling, then affix
the whole Qur'an in flowing letters and fine calligraphy
around the walls and doors, and inside and outside in pewter and
     porphyry
clear enough to read. Then colonnades threading out through gardens
laid out in patterns among lakes and fountains
where water always flows
no matter where the Princess goes,
a constant gurgling sound, the trickling and gushing
of water. Then places to do the ritual washing
before the prayer, and on one side, a great mosque.
There it should be simple. High ceiling, don't ask
your army of worker jinn to put gold or jewels here.

It should be a space that is totally open and clear
for prayer. Then bed-chambers, wooden chests
carved and decorated with finest
workmanship. High windows everywhere,
and in the main hall, there must be twenty-four
encrusted with diamonds and pearls. That hall should be simply
    celestial. You must feel you are
bathed in pure starlight. You should see far, far
into space, the roof should be an observatory, the heavens revolving
    with their planetary spheres
to be watched and charted throughout the years.
At our feet, the earth. Trees and mosses reproduced
in thick carpeting, and rivulets everywhere sluiced
in runnels and channels, even in the main hall.
But above, the sky, that great dome, the sun, that gassy ball,
visible and shedding its rays
on our human days.
Of course, a quick roof can be covered over if too hot.

Then kitchens filled with servants to cook food for the whole lot
of townspeople who will come every day to be fed,
the main doors should be wide open, the beggars and poor people
    and orphans led
to a dining hall large enough for elephants.
A great parquet floor with hundreds of low, round tables, no sense
in being lavish with the palace but forgetting generosity.
Such greed is what transforms humankind into the worst monstrosity
ever to walk on the planet.
Then I want you to get
the best cooks, and fill the gardens with wheat
and fruit and vegetables, the pens with bleat-

ing sheep for mutton, camels in the courtyard
munching and grumbling, no lard
anywhere, naturally, but finest things growing seasonally
to make the people healthy.
Storehouses, stables filled with great stallions fit for battles,
sleek runners, swift as clouds, with well-wrought leather saddles.
And hunting falcons, sharp-eyed, sharp-beaked, swift,
to sit on a leather glove, then drift
off on a wheeling flight
that brings the prey within sight.
Swoop fast, kill and fly with it back.
There is nothing like a falcon, so noble, its attack
is pure, it dives like a dart from Allah! Wings spread,
its eyes able to spot the eyes in a rabbit's head.
*Go!* That is enough. But all before dawn!"
The jinn left. Ala-udeen had to suppress a yawn
he was so exhausted. He slept.

At daybreak the jinn came and swept
him off to see the sunlit palace.
The gold light of the sun threw pale gold lines like a spun-glass chalice
onto the transparency of the outer walls.
It loomed on its fortress foundations, tall on its round hill, its inner
    halls
still freshly sparkling as from dew
from the jinn's work all night, done in such few
hours. It outdid Ala-udeen's wildest wishes
everywhere he went, from the diamond-studded domes to the
    wriggling goldfishes
in the hundreds of ponds and lakes,
and in the kitchens white-aproned servants making thousands of

pancakes
to be served in celebration.
It had nothing to do with the world of economic collapse or global
    inflation.
It shone on its hilltop like a perfect globe of water on the petal of a
    rose at dawn.
In this world, there was nothing anywhere like it the sun has ever
    shone on.

One added detail:
Ala-udeen had also not failed
to instruct the jinn to lay a long carpet to provide
a path from the sultan's palace to his own for his new bride
to walk on.
It unrolled down the hill and across the garden like dark green velvet
    lawn
and went from door to door. This was her suspension bridge.
It was to take her from her father's family heritage
to her new husband's, so she also would be new.
She would leave all childhood behind, the court's over-protectiveness,
    she would now be her own woman, baby-blue
changing to the rich royal purples of womanly dignity
on the high round hill above the city.
Ala-udeen sent his mother with her servants and retinue
to the sultan's palace to tell the Princess, "You
are invited this night to Ala-udeen's palace,"
where she would be in a wonderland far more extravagant than
    that of Alice.
Meanwhile, the sultan had left his golden bed
that rose like a pyramid with tiger-claw legs on its regal bedstead
far from how our Prophet Muhammad used to sleep,

peace be upon him, on the floor on rush matting, the rushes making
    deep
marks on his body while he slept.
For he slept as a servant sleeps, and always kept
himself low, when most men want to be high.
Man falls to great depths when he overreaches for the uppermost sky.

So the sultan got up and went to his window and what he saw
made his jaw
drop. On the bare hill of yesterday
stood a castle fortress in full display
like the crown on the bald head of a king.
It covered the whole hill in the fresh morning sunlight, sparkling.
"How did he do it?" he asked aloud, alone.
"That palace looks like it's been there for centuries of stone
and brickwork, latticework, gardens, hedges, pathways,
though it's only been there for a few days…"
Then he suddenly remembered! Such time had not passed. Only
    *one night!* There was no way
it could have been, nail by nail and rock by rock, hammered  into
    place.
It stood there like a flying saucer recently arrived from outer space.
A knock on the door. A messenger.
"The mother of Ala-udeen, your new son-in-law, sir,
awaits you
with her retinue
in the Throne Room."
He put on his costliest bathrobe and his turban with the eagle-plume,
and went to the audience.
She bowed low in obedience,
servants standing silently around her, dressed

in a robe so fine and so full of tiny pearls, he was sure she was especially
    blessed
by Allah to be so well taken care of by her son.
She had come to announce Ala-udeen's invitation
for his daughter to join him in his own palace that night.
There would be festivities and fireworks, and a release of doves' flight.

Ala-udeen left his house in the donkey stable forever.
He rode on his white horse through the streets, sever-
ing all connection with his father's house.
(It is said it is now inhabited by one mouse,
one cricket, a blackbird family and a praying mantis
who cocks his intelligent head from side to side as it waits to plant on an
    insect the kiss
of death.) And the Princess also
left her house that night, and walked slow-
ly across the garden on the carpet,
up the hill, across a new parapet
and a bridge, winding up
the hill sup-
plied with servants each carrying candles
in candlesticks fitted with diamond handles,
until she entered the hall, and there
saw Ala-udeen, lively as daylight, on a small stair
in a richly carpeted corner, cushions
piled against the wall, musicians
playing ouds in melodious unison behind a screen.

"I present myself," she said, "to my husband, Ala-udeen."

So a fresh breath of life spread throughout the town.

Ala-udeen was never condescending, he didn't look down
on people. It was true as he had vowed,
the palace was always filled with the poor and the overpow-
ered folk of the world, banquets for the blind and festivities for
    orphans.
No one left his walls without gold coins, not in one's
or two's, but whole bagfuls, bulging,
in remembrance of the time he had left the garden after indulging
himself by stuffing his pockets full of fruit.
Now his generosity was absolute.
For he knew where it came from.
He didn't hold onto some
and let other flow.
He let it all go.
For he knew that the lamp on the shelf in his private bedroom,
    and the ring on his finger, were both gifts that came directly
    from Allah. ...Time passed,
and clouds like golden boats passed
the turrets and towers of their scintillating castle.

It was purity, it was light, it was like the diamond-clear atoms
    of the manifest world.
Perfect patterns that beamed out the Names and Attributes of Allah,
    openly unfurled.
And it was good, for Ala-udeen and Badroulbadour
were generous and compassionate, and in their hearts they were pure.

But Allah set up the creation in opposites.
When there's light, darkness rushes to meet it, and it all fits
together in a circle like night sliding off gradually into day.
So all this light must be tested by darkness. There's nothing wrong.

It's just the way
Allah has set it up. So we always must turn to Him.
He gets jealous if we love this world too much, for then our chances
    of seeing Him are slim.

So the old magician in Africa woke up one day on cue,
threw off his moldy blankets, snorted and coughed, his face was blue,
his nose was purple, his drooping eyes were green.
His hair was like wire, he was gnarled and twisted, the worst thing
    you've ever seen.
He'd been working his normal hocus-pocus,
but his powers had somehow gone out of focus.
He couldn't vanish at will, or make man and wife suddenly hate.
He decided he would have to do something quick before it was
    too late.
"If only I had some really super-power, with a jinn to do my bidding!"
 He drew some magic circles in the dust, but they only sat there
    as if he'd been kidding.
"A jinn to help me, I'm getting old, now I have to be extra crafty."
Then he went to the window to close it, for the African nights get
    drafty,
and when he closed the wooden shutter he thought of that wooden
    trap-door in the ground
with the brass ring that gleamed and extended so round
that it could be pulled and opened, lifted clean.

It was then he remembered Ala-udeen!

He consulted his books. He wanted to find out
if that boy he had left underground had gotten out
or was now just a pile of bones.

He rummaged around in his laboratory full of voodoo-dolls and clones,
a real horror. He mumbled and muttered
as his scaly fingers turned the pages, candles sputtered
to fill out the bleakness of this atmosphere
in his damp hole full of queer
amulets and things tied with thong.

He was the incarnation of everything that was wrong.
He drew diagrams. He burned incense. He threw coins.
Finally he saw by his magic that beauty and abundance was bursting
    from the loins
of Ala-udeen in sons and wealth and generosity.
So he put on his stinky felt hat and coat, his mind full of animosity,
and flew through the sky to China.
No light could possibly shine
upon his schemes.

But man schemes and Allah schemes.
And Allah is the best of schemers.
Rays of definite hard-edged light come to wake up dreamers.

"That lamp!" he said through his yellow teeth, "I must get it!
There would have been no way for Ala-udeen to be so great before
    he met it
in the garden as I instructed him. I must get in
to the palace. *I must get it!*"
He was totally obsessed. He couldn't forget it
as he landed in Canton or Peking or wherever it was they lived.
"I will make this magnificence pass from his fingers like water
    through a sieve,"
he said to himself, hunched under his personal black cloud.

He moved into town among the people as if a black shroud
hung around him.
Crowds of people shrunk away from him.

So against Ala-udeen's bright light came dark cloud.
The magician scowled into the face of that light and laughed out loud.
He took a room in a dingy hotel,
he moved among people with a stingy smell,
as of usury, faintly sulfurous, finding out, CIA'ing what he could,
until some man informed him that Ala-udeen had gone hunting
    with his hawks for eight days in a distant wood.
So he went to his hovel,
chuckling as he shoved
the door open, "Good, good," wringing his hands,
then consulting crystal balls and muttering dark commands,
he found that the secret lamp that brought such glory to its owner
was not with Ala-udeen, but in the palace in a corner
of his private bedroom. No sooner
did he find this highly sensitive piece of information out
than he let out a shrieky shout
of uncontained glee,
and then whispered hoarsely, "Soon that lamp will belong to *me!*"

Next morning, he went to the coppersmith's stall
in the marketplace, and bought all
twelve of the new lamps sitting on the shelf,
then put them in a basket, feeling quite proud of himself,
with his infallible plan that would not fail.
As he approached Ala-udeen's palace, across the garden from the
    sultan's, he began to wail
in a high-pitched voice that rattled the windows and goblets of gold:

*"New lamps for old! I say, I'll exchange shiny new lamps for old!"*
What a cheat! What a master deception!
He would give you a new lamp if you gave him an old one, with no
    objection
at being given something less.
But no one around him was able to guess
the deep darkness of his evil intention.
And that old fossil didn't mention
it to anyone.
Children danced around him, making fun
of this stranger who shouted *"New lamps for old."* "He's a fool," they
    said,
"a nut-case," "cuckoo," "he's out of his head,"
"he's flown the coop!" They didn't see
the cunning gleam in his shifty eye.

He stood outside the palace below the delicate window,
and the Princess was attracted to glance out to see what the hubbub
    below
was all about.
"Go see what that noise is all about,"
she said to one of her servants.
The girl came back giggling. "It makes no sense.
He says he'll give new lamps for any old ones,
tin, or silver, or even tarnished gold ones."

Now for safety's sake, Ala-udeen had never shown the Princess the lamp,
feeling that the less known it was the less chance of a major cramp
in its miraculous usefulness whenever it was needed.
It wasn't distrust, for she was, in all her innocence having been so
    carefully protected,

brilliant in everything except the vile ways of the world. Never
    infected
herself with dark or conniving thoughts, to her everything positively
    smiled
and she was therefore less able to detect the omnivorous wiles
of evil in the world.

So it was really not her fault that the sudden idea in her mind unfurled
and she cried out: *"Wait!* There's one in Ala-udeen's room on a shelf.
It's horribly old and battered," The Princess said: "I'll go there myself
and get it!" She laughed and danced down the hall.
She had absolutely no idea at all
what that lamp was. To her it was a dusty antique perhaps, nothing
special, nothing to freeze
forever as castle decor. She'd get something new to please
Ala-udeen when he returned.

When the servant brought it to the door, the magician's eyes burned
in their sockets like two sunken coals about to explode.
He snatched it from her hands, thrust it deep into his coat, and
    dropped the whole load
of new lamps at the door. *"Take them all!"*

"Why, that man is quite crazy," she said, as she saw them fall
in a clanking heap.
They shone, all polished, quite brilliantly. "I guess we can keep
them all..."

The magician ran down the street, past the coppersmith's stall,
past the city gates, out down the road, past the forest,
he ran and ran, then finally sat to rest

on a dark hill waiting for twilight.

A hoot-owl's forlorn moan announced the night.

The magician hunched over the lamp, squinting,
covered in shadows, damp leaves glinting
eerily in the moonlight as they drifted down.

The magician took the lamp from his coat and set it down
on his knee.

He rubbed it slowly.
The jinn shot up from its depths, taller than a cypress tree.
His fierce head loomed in the night, and he chanted boomingly:

> *"Your wish is my command,*
> *in whoever's hand*
> *the lamp may be in,*
> *for I and the other jinn*
> *are only slaves, and we obey.*
> *So, master, ask without delay!"*

The magician snarled out his command.
He was so monstrous that he couldn't stop his hand
from shaking.

The jinn hovered there, the black, now unlit sky quaking
with intensity,
the airless air all around him shrinking from its normal immensity.

"Take that palace you built for Ala-udeen,

take it with the Princess inside, and transport it, with all its clean
sheets, its gold trays, its stallions, its jewels,
take it and carry it to Africa!" He fairly drooled
with evil. But the jinn obeyed anyone in whose hands
the lamp was in, so the palace and the Princess, sailing over orient lands
invisibly, flew faster than a turbojet supersonic Concorde
from China to Africa, where, like a sword
slicing down through the air,
it landed quietly near a fair
oasis.

The landing didn't even wake up the Princess.

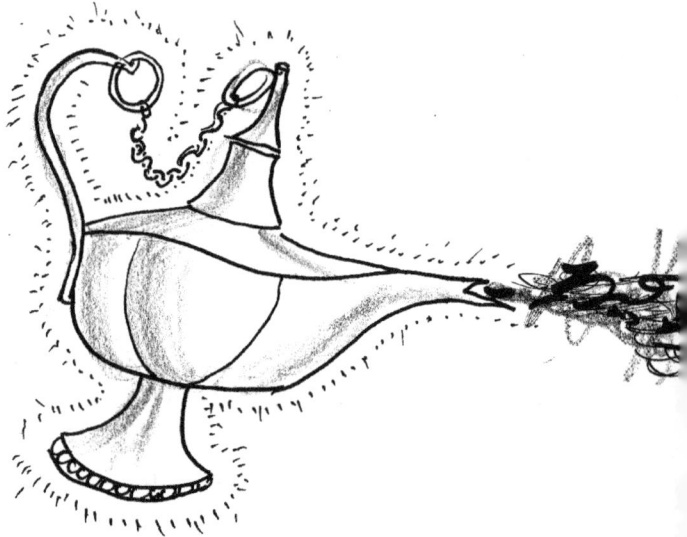

## CHAPTER 5: THE EMPTY HILL, THE RIVER, AND THE RING

Every morning for many years the Sultan would go to his window
after his prayers, and standing with his palms on the windowsill, slowly go
parapet by parapet, and turret by turret
over the lovely vision of Ala-udeen's palace, to savor it.

So what a surprise jolted him as he stood there to see
the round hill was now empty!
Nothing. No stone or glitter,
just the usual rapid wing-flutter and twitter
of dawn's breakfasting birds.
No shadow or hole, no crater, no nothing, it was absurd
but true.
*The palace had vanished into the blue!*

He sent troops. They could find not a hair.
There was no evidence of palace on that hill anywhere.
He sent troops to the woods where his son-in-law hunted
and had him brought back in chains, for he now suspected
Ala-udeen of magic, and that he made his palace vanish
in the same way he had made it suddenly appear in its Arabo-Spanish
splendor.
*"You are nothing but a palace lender!"*

But what is more important,
*you've stolen my daughter!* This fact makes me regret the time I've spent
loving you. No, there is nothing to say.
You will have your head cut off at the neck without delay!"

So Ala-udeen lay in prison confused to his bones.
There was no reason at all for the sultan to talk to him in such terrible
      tones.
What had he done?
But soon everyone
in town who had been given things,
seven course dinners, gold coins, rings
and fine thoroughbred horses
called for his release, thousands calling on the sultan's forces
of mercy to please
let him go. So Ala-udeen tried to be at ease
at the sultan's feet and said, "Oh please, sir,
what have I done to you to stir
such wrath?" *"You mean you don't know?"*
"No." "Well, come here then, and I will gladly show
you your crime."

Ala-udeen saw the empty hill for the first time.
His heart sank. His knees buckled. He fell.
He fainted. There is no way to tell
what it was that was taken away in his heart.
It was as if Allah had removed its most beautiful part.

He stayed unconscious for days.
Then finally awoke, slowly, expressing his amaze-
ment "I *will* find her, I *will* find her," he said, "just give me forty days!"

He didn't know what he would do. He had no lamp, but there must
     be ways
to find a vanished palace?

"Just forty," the sultan answered, "that's all. After that it's malice
in your intention, and theft we have to charge you with, that you're
     a cunning, unscrupulous magician
who makes apparitions of palaces appear to trap innocent princesses in.
After forty days, if she's not back, it's your head that will fall!"
And with that he frowned and turned and walked quickly out
     of the hall.

So Ala-udeen began the search.
He went to the hill. He perched
on its cliffs where great stones had stood so recently
to see if he could possibly see
any traces, nails, screws, cut blocks, steel girders.
There was truly not even the shadow of a hair. It was absurd!

He couldn't believe it. Yet he saw how quickly it had come,
the jeweled halls, the ponds, the sump-
tuous… *everything about it*, abundance abounding,
both its appearance and its disappearance, absolutely astounding!

"Flimsy threads," he repeated to himself, "we hang,
and the whole creation hangs by flimsy threads. It's thanks
to the mercy of Allah to let us *be* at all!"

But his grief for the vanishing Princess almost made him fall
dizzily from the cliff-edge
until he clutched a hedge

and was saved. He wandered around the city asking everyone
he had known and been generous to if anyone
had seen his palace. They laughed at him. Now worthless
as they were, they considered him even less
than they were, and just jeered at him.
Some of the sultan's men even sneered at him.
Down dusty alleys, going on a hunch, checking out clues,
stopping everyone with, "Have *you* seen my palace?" but it only
    amused
them. He was so full of desperation, so out of his head, he stepped
    right out of time and space
and was bang in another century in a totally different place.

He was found sitting by himself in a lonely American 24-hour café
somewhere down around 3rd and Broadway.
To everyone he was just another sullen Chinese youth,
drinking green tea from a porcelain cup in a dark restaurant booth
although his clothes were a bit odd.
He didn't know who to ask here, the whole mod-
ern frantic maze of traffic and people so overwhelmed him,
he felt he was trapped in a jungle-gym
unable to get out.

He put on a tie and coat
and asked people, *"Where* is my palace?" much to their surprise and
    pity.
He wandered this way for days in both the inner and outer city,
just another "nut." But he also went heartbrokenly back in time
and found himself in the sublime
company of what evolution-theory anthropologists call "Stone-Age
    Neanderthal"

but who were in no way primitive at all,
but illuminated, transparent giants sitting around an incandescent
glow.
"Oh *where,*" Ala-udeen asked, standing among them, "is my palace?
Please, sirs, *I want to know!*"
Their gentle laughter reverberated through all the prehistoric ages.
Their cool coal-black eyes and shining teeth and smiles showed they
were sages
harmonized with biospheric conditions.

His passionate trek led him into and out of various time-and-space
situations.
He was dazed. He was confused. This flash-card universe made him
stutter.
He went to a modern metropolis and bought a computer
to work out all the data: time, place, number of jewels,
how many horses in the stables, what kinds of tools
had made the shimmering glass archways gleam.

He hired helicopters and flew in a team
over the area, back and forth. No result.
He took heat-scans, had physicists measure the soil content for melt-
out or any sudden change. But everything only conclusively proved
that in fact nothing had ever even been removed
because *it had never existed!*

Ala-udeen's eyes misted
over. He trudged through the streets of China.
He went out alone, undone, bereft, hands and pockets empty, to find a
place to reflect. He wandered as far as the river, and there
he bent out over the water to stare

at something that really shocked him.

There was a figure, same clothes, same hat-brim,
same face as his, or he assumed it was, for it had changed.
Pale, sunken cheeks, dark circles under his eyes, he looked deranged
to himself as his face-rippled in the river-water's flow.
And at that moment he saw that everything in this universe has to go
with the total current downstream.
Rippling, shimmering, wavering as in a dream
he had to wake up out of.

As he reflected on his reflection, something began to shove
its way through his momentary madness.

He did *wudhu,* quickly, briskly, it splashed away sadness,
he stood, and bowed, prostrated and prayed
to Allah for help, then went back after wiping his face the usual way
to look at that face of his again in the stream.
He leaned way out over the water holding onto a green
stem that broke. He fell, and as he clutched at anything
and caught hold of a rock, he happened to rub the magic ring
still on his finger. *Suddenly a red mushroom cloud!*

It rose above the river! It frightened away a whole crowd
of jabbering blue jays. The jinn appeared,
his immensely tall and distant head just cleared
the forest at the water's edge.
Ala-udeen clambered back up onto the river bank's grassy ledge.

> *"Your wish is my command*
> *in whoever's hand*

*the ring may be on,*
*for I and the other Jinn*
*are only slaves, and we obey.*
*So, master, ask without delay!"*

"Dear jinn, please save me from this black hole I am in
and bring back the palace to me built by you and the other jinn!"
"But, master," he said deeply bowing,
"I am only the jinn of the ring.
You must ask the jinn of the lamp to return your palace."
Ala-udeen then looked at him without any malice
at all in his eyes, and said, "Then please, if you can,
transport me to where it stands!"

In a fraction of a flash
he was flown in the jinn's flying sash
across the sky to the African plain.
Date palms brushed their spiky fronds, no rain
had fallen, the air was burning hot,
sweet-smelling, dry. Ala-udeen got
up from where he landed and found himself standing under the
    palace window.

Just at that moment the Princess happened to glance down below
as he stood up. Their glances met.
A flash of lightning lit up between them brighter than any they had
    seen yet.
Ala-udeen came up the back staircase, and she took him into the
    main hall.
Nothing had changed at all.
The pillows in their usual positions,

the chests and couches, the velvet cushions
and freely roaming panthers,
ferns, gardens out the windows, antlers
of stags visible through the bushes of the hedge...

This palace as it always was, shimmering as always just on the edge
of non-existence. The two wept with happiness and relief.
This reunion, after the sudden disappearance, completely
    restored their belief.

"Oh wife, where is the lamp? The old, battered copper one standing
    on my bedroom shelf?"
She wept. *"I knew that was it!* It was my fault, really. I ran and got it
    myself
to trade in for a new one from that old man
so you would find it and be pleased with me. He snatched it and ran
off and since then I've been here
in Africa, a prisoner!"

"Where does he keep it?" "In his shirt, I know because he showed it
    to me
one day all of a sudden pulling it out of his shirt and chuckling
    triumphantly.
I hate him. He's so mean!  And smells of brimstone and sulfur!"

"Well, be patient a little longer. I've got a plan to get us out of here.
You must change your tune. You must greet him sweetly.
Invite him to your room. Put makeup on and dress beautifully
for him. Say you've changed your mind.
You've decided I *am* dead. You've been totally blind.
Now you want to sit and eat, and drink sherbet with him.

Then exchange goblets. That will certainly woo him.
I will be back in an hour with what you've got to pour
into that golden goblet of yours
before you serve it to him." He ran out and down the stairs, carefully
watching for the magician, crept along the palace-wall, deftly
stepping from shadow to shadow,
then down a dusty road until he got to market row
and found a druggist selling herbs and dried potions and powders.

"I want something that kills, but tastes like nothing. No pills, no
    poisonous tooth-powder,
but something that dissolves completely
and makes sweet drinks taste even more sweetly."
The druggest cocked a squint eye.
"I've got just the right thing, but the price is quite high."
Ala-udeen was in rags. But he had one gold coin.
"Sold!" the druggist cried. "Whoever drinks this will soon join
his ancestors in the next world."

So Ala-udeen ran back, and with "*Bismillah*," he hurled
all the invisible powder
into the fizzy crowd of
sherbet bubbles frothing in the glass.
"When he drinks this, the old magician will pass
out of existence.

Now, have you girls that dance,
musicians that pluck, songs to sing?
You must present everything
as if you are welcoming him as a groom.
Then when he drinks it and falls backwards, *call me to your room!*"

Ala-udeen hid in the cellar.
The moment came. The old man with his yellow
grin and black cloak came in and found,
to his utter amazement, that instead of round
pouting lips saying, *"No!"*
the Princess was inviting him to go
to her private rooms that very night.

When he entered them through gauzy curtains, he was greeted by
    the sight
of servants with huge fronds for fanning,
and a low table with two sherbet goblets brilliantly shining,
and sheep-skins and carpets flung around on the floor for him
    to sit on.

He was convinced of her change of heart when she beckoned him
    to sit on
the floor next to her,
and she raised the sher-
bet glasses in the air. "Wait," she said, "before you drink!
Why don't we exchange glasses, so that we sip from each other's?
    *Hmmmmm*, dear man, what do you think?"

His viscious eye gleamed yellow. He smiled,
and all the grotesqueness of his evil guile
came out when he tried to be romantic. She stared, horrified.
It was the *nafs*. Everything in the *nafs* is horrid, terrified
by the light of pure spirit. He grinned.
It was raw *nafs*, thin-
ly veiled now, facing the moon-like face of the Princess
who was spiritual light in human dress.

All his activity, from the first of our story,
comes from the *nafs*. Magic manipulations, gory
ulterior motives, yet without him,
without our *nafs* magician,
there would have been
no lamp. Without the means
the end would have escaped us. This means
that by the *nafs* we're created in, we
travel to the Light of Allah, He

Whose Light is the Light of the heavens and the earth.
The only goal worth
having.

So he took the goblet offered to him, slavering
and gulped it down.
His face turned purple. He clutched his sides. A black frown
blacker than pitch crossed his brow,
then he fell back. The poison didn't even allow
one moment to pass before
he was thrown to the floor.

Ala-udeen was called for.
He ran up the stair.
The Princess embraced him. He said, "Now, let me finish this affair
and get our palace back to where it belongs.
So please, send the servants, and the singers of songs,
into the next roam to wait,
and before too long we can anticipate
that we will be back in China.

Tbe Princess stood back as he rushed to the dead man. He opened
    his shirt and saw the shine
of the lamp, and when he had pulled it out, he rubbed it.
Within a fraction of a fraction of a moment he had dubbed it
a total success. *Al-hamdulillah*!
The Princess' eyes grew wide as before them tall as a mountain stood
    the jinn, the slave of Allah.

> *"Your wish is my command,*
> *in whoever's hand*
> *the lamp may be in,*
> *for I and the other jinn*
> *are only slaves, and we obey.*
> *So, master, ask without delay."*

Next morning the sultan performed his dawn prayer as usual,
recited *"Ya Seen"* for his daughter whom he thought was dead, refused
    all
food again for the twenty-fourth day in a row
then went across the room with shoulders sloping low
in sorrow for his daughter's and the palace's disappearance.

For this heartbreak had changed him, had brought him low, both his
    inside and his outside appearance,
and his inner light had grown bigger although his body was thinner
since he could no longer eat, neither breakfast, nor lunch, nor dinner.
And his greed for splendor stopped. Jewels that glittered no longer
    interested him,
but reciting Qur'an all day — instead, sober and even grim
reflection rather than laughter and endless wealth.
Allah was changing the sultan by His own Masterly stealth.

So the sultan went weeping to the window to look out on the
      empty hilltop,
but when he saw with his own eyes what stood there, he had to stop
dead in his tracks. He shouted out in wonder and amaze-
ment, "*Allahu akbar!* This is crazy!
Am I seeing things or not?
Is that Ala-udeen's old palace on the topmost spot
of the hill?"

He blinked his eyes. But the palace, though shimmering, stood there
      still.

He ordered his horse, put on his robes and galloped across the bridge
and urged his horse up the hillside road, and rode along the ridge
just approaching the gate.

Both Ala-udeen and the Princess were there already, wait-
ing. They all embraced. Then they led the sultan into the sunken
      chandelier hall.
They served him ices, sat under sunlight, then starlight, and told him
      all
the details of everything:
the lamp, the magician, the jinn in the ring.
They watched the stars as they fled like lances
in their fiery dances
across the sky.

Time seemed to stop as they found themselves again together
      without that sly
magician lurking in the shadows behind them.

"For a moment this palace and all its riches are with us," said the sultan.

"But at any moment it might all disappear again," said Ala-udeen, "so thank Allah for the breaths we've got, after what we've seen!"

*Al-hamdulillah wa shukrulillah* could be heard solemnly sounding through those halls.

And so this story goes flowing to its final conclusion like a barrel down Niagara falls.

## EPILOGUE: IF YOU THOUGHT THE STORY WAS OVER, IT IS NOT

The nasty old magician naturally had a nastier brother.
You would say they had a cruel father and mother,
to have been so nasty, but maybe not.
It is only by the decree of Allah that some are good, and some are rotten to the core.

Anyway, this brother hadn't received any news from his brother
      where before
a post-card or a telepathic call would come at least once a week.
So now, throwing coins, consulting crystal balls, he began to seek
the reason for this recent silence.
"Perhaps he had met with violence."
Suddenly, at a shift of signs, a death card or shadow in the crystal,
he saw China, a body in the ground, not from hijack or kidnap or
      pistol,
but poisonous powder, and then that nasty brother began to perspire
because he saw that the spirit of his less nasty brother was being
      *fried in the Fire!*
But rather than frighten
him it only tightened him
in his intention to track down the killer and take absolute revenge,
even if it meant ransacking Rome again or stalking him among
      the stones of Stonehenge.
So he consulted his thick book, did horoscopes, fiddled with charms,

until a clear picture emerged of 'Ala ud-Deen happy in the arms
of bliss, Allah's generosity, and his wife.
"I will get into that palace and end that no-good magician-killer's life!"
He sped to Peking and took a room in a run-down no-star hotel.
He spent a week or two slinking around in the streets until he began
    to smell
a way to dupe Ala-udeen and further his sinister plan.

He heard of a lady saint, an old woman full of miracles, more
    generous than
the generous wind that blows seeds in their pine-cones to the ground.
So he found out where she lived, everyone knew, and he began to follow
    her around
as she healed people, fed people, helped people secretly and out in
    the open.
Everyone knew her and wept when they were near her, she was a
    *waliyya*, purer than
a spring of silvery water.
But it was part of her destiny that he got her.

So one night, that hell-bent man followed her veil-wrapped form
as she made her way home in black robes and barefoot, walking her
    norm-
al route, and he grabbed her and tied her up and pulled her —
not knowing that at that very moment the Light of Allah filled her —
down into a dingy basement where he tied her to a pipe
while her heart was filled with *alhamdulillah* that she was perhaps now
    ripe
to go to Allah since she was ready at any time if called.
Although the evil brother would at his death be hellishly enthralled.
(What he lacked in magical subtlety

he more than made up for in cruelty!)

Then this gnarled wretch bought some black robes and black veils
and smeared grease-paint on his face so his male
identity would vanish completely
and he could masquerade as this saintly woman sweetly
soothing the multitudes, her *tasbih* beads hanging around her neck.
He could not see then that his own life would soon smash on Allah's
     rocks, a shipwreck.
His own time was running out!

He wrapped himself well, just his beady eyes peering out
over the top of his veil,
and he affected a high female
lilt to his voice, a soft whisper of modest humility,
then made his way to the street below the palace in the center of the city
surrounded, unlike his brother had been, by a crowd of the weeping poor.
They called on the saintly woman to chase their woes from their door
and make them well again.
They did not know that this was the worst of men.

By Allah, just at that moment, as before, the Princess happened to look
out her window at the scene, then she took
one of her servants aside and asked who it was in the black robes below
     who was passing by the palace wall.
"That is no ordinary woman at all,"
the servant said, not knowing how truly she spoke. "That saintly lady is
     able to cure the ill
of any leper, any feverish child or cripple
and does more things for Allah people don't even talk about.
She's a great *waliyya!* She hardly ever goes out

of her private chamber where she's always doing prayers
and *dhikr*, managing the affairs
of people who are unable to manage their own."
"Oh go get her, please," the Princess pleaded, "I so want to be shown
the spiritual path, the way to Allah through *dhikr* and prayer and
 fasting!"
(Again, to move this story along, our dear Princess must be perfectly
 trusting.)
So the servant went down to the street and approached the robed form,
 and after asking
if she would be so kind as to come upstairs to the palace for just a
 moment,
the old man's brother, with sweet soft words, all veiled, said, "You must
 have been sent
by Allah. Why this is too great an honor for a humble woman like me!"
And she was brought to the Princess who greeted her by embracing her
 warmly,
his greenish gleaming eye then invisible.
He pulled the veil across as if permissible
to be seen only by Allah, alone,
his cruel heart hard as stone.

The Princess asked "her" to please stay and teach her the Path.
"But I must stay secluded, to pray and fast, or the wrath
of my Lord will thunder on me."
The poor Princess fell for it, wonderingly.
But her innocent heart's not to blame.
She was all moon-rays, and had never been singed by the black flame
of hatred that consumes some men's hearts with its smoke.
She had no way of guessing that this monster was playing a joke
in order to kill Ala-udeen.

Instead, she led the "saint" to a room behind a screen
with mother of pearl and gold tigers inlaid upon it,
where "she" could be alone and pray, and come out from time to time
    and recite Qur'anic
phrases to guide and instruct her
in the unfolding of her inner flower.

She would not eat in the Princess's presence, she said she was too lowly to
    share the same space,
but the fact was that the magician was afraid to show the Princess his face.
Later they chatted. They sat in a corner in the most lavish hall of the
    palace.
"What do you think of this room, Oh saintly woman," said the Princess,
    (sipping from a chalice
some health drink with chamomile flowers and some particularly sour
    vitamins
the "saint" had said she should first drink down before she could possibly
    be invited in.
"Your vibrations are too strong for me," the criminal had said to her,
    whisperingly).

"Well," said the bent black form, scanning the room with a veiled eye,
"it is most impressive, really it is, but it needs just one thing hanging high
in the middle of the hall to make it completely perfect."
"What is that, oh divine woman? Tell me. I have inspect-
ed each cranny of pearl and amethyst and never found imperfection."
"A roc's egg," said the scoundrel, "it would be the right injection
of color and smooth form and something oval suspended in the air above
    our heads."
"What is a roc?" asked the innocent Princess, turning away from the
    dead

eyes hidden in the black veil to look at the hall as vast as it was wide.
"A roc is a gigantic bird, my dear, that builds its nest on the highest
    mountainside
in the visible world."
"I shall ask my husband tonight," she said, as her thoughts curled
around the idea. So pure a thing
suspended on a swing
of silver.

The magician was so pleased he didn't notice the wooden sliver
from the *tasbih* beads enter his index finger.
He was filled with evil glee as he went back to his room as the Qur'an
    singer
began to recite
at the coming-on of night.

"Ala-udeen," the Princess said, in a low voice slightly tinged with gloom.
"I always thought that this palace was perfect, especially the main room
with its twenty-four windows of pearls, and diamonds and tiny
    studded rubies.
But now I think it needs one thing more to be really of incomparable
    beauty."
"Tell me, Princess, and *insha'Allah* I will get it for you without delay."
"A roc's egg," she replied, and he left her side without say-
ing a word, and rose up the stairs to his room where he pulled the lamp
    from his shirt.
He rubbed the place that was always rubbed, the same spot where his
    mother rubbed off the dirt.
Clouds rolled, smoke boiled, gold light shot like geysers.
The giant shot, arms folded, up in multiplying sizes.

*Your wish is my command,*
*in whoever's hand*
*the lamp may be in,*
*for I and the other jinn*
*are only slaves, and we obey.*
*So, master, ask without delay."*

"Oh jinn, please, bring a roc's egg to be hung from the palace ceiling."

But this time, instead of a low bow, suddenly the whole world went
    reeling
in wild circles, thunder cracked, lightning flashed, the floor shook like
    the train-track of doom.
Smoke thick as ink and air deep as water filled Ala-udeen's small room.
The jinn frowned like an oxen, his huge face was glowering and fierce.
His eyes burned like two fiery coals with a glance that could pierce
iron. "You have asked and I've obeyed.
But now you want me to convey
my earthly master to be hung like a decoration from your roof.
This deserves that you, the Princess and the palace should be ground to a
    fine powder beneath the hoof
of a snarling monster. *No! A thousand times No!* I will never bring what
    you want.
But in fact," calming down now, "this request is not yours, but from an
    evil spy plant-
ed within these walls.
Take care, Ala-udeen, for this murderer stalks you, disguised as a holy
    woman, through the halls
of the palace. It's the brother of that magician
from Africa, a vision
of the fires of Hell could not be blacker.

Don't let him deceive you, be on your guard against a silent attacker!"

With these words the jinn disappeared in the lamp and the smoke hung
for a second.

Then the air cleared, and Ala-udeen went down to the Princess to reckon
with this pious imposter.

He would show who was master.

*"La howla wa la quwata ila billahi 'ali al-atheem —*

*Insha'Allah,* by the power of Allah, I will reduce this black spot to white
cream!

There was no time to tell her eveything, so when he came to the Princess
he complained of a distress
on the top of his head.

"Oh dear husband, listen. There is a healer here, a saintly woman," she
said.

"She will touch you with her hand and you'll be cured."

*"That magician's brother will wish he were insured*

*when I get done with him,"* he thought.

"Perhaps she can help me," he said. "Why don't you call for her, and I
will show her the spot

that hurts." So the Princess got up and went to the room behind the
screen,

and when that black form entered, he saw Ala-udeen

stand up, saying he had a headache, and pointing to a place on his skull.

"I've heard, good woman, that you've a touch that makes dull
headaches disappear.

Well I've got one now. Perhaps, with Allah's help, you would touch me
here,"

and so saying approached, as the saintly woman approached, a glint of
dagger flashing from his robe.

Ala-udeen jumped up, and with a swift upper kick, faster than a strobe-light kicked the dagger right out from his hand.

Ala-udeen leapt once, and with a quick twist land-

ed on top of him, knocked him to the floor, had the dagger

which he'd caught in the air when he leapt, the magician tried to stagger

to his feet, he roared a mighty roar,

bucked terrifically, as if he were a wild boar

held down by hounds, he was strong,

he backed out, it was not time for Ala-udeen to make a wrong

move, so he listened in his heart for Allah's word,

he said *"Allah"* on his tongue aloud, and with absurd

speed landed him a blow on the chin with his foot

since, for a split-second, the magician's brother had been distracted by the
sliver in his index-finger put

there by Allah, and Ala-udeen plunged the knife down into his back as if it
were a bag of black soot,

and it went right through his heart.

He died, quick victim of God's dart.

*A dead avenger!*

"What have you done?" the Princess cried, "she was no danger!"

"She was no saint!" said Ala-udeen cool as ice.

"It was that black magician's brother, disguised as a saint, pretending
to be nice

so he could get into the palace and kill me."

"Oh Ala-udeen, forgive me! *Alhamdulillah* you're alive! These close-calls
don't thrill me."


With the jinn's help they found the real saintly woman and freed her

and she taught the Princess and Ala-udeen the Path to Allah, and they
traveled it speedier

than they might have without her elegant instructions.

Such is the way of the saintly ones and Allah's soverign protections.

And so twice the dark cloud of *nafs* in all its flimsiness had tried to take
    the owner of the lamp.
But it is only owned by Allah, and His Light is greater than any earthly
    manifest wattage or amp.

In its place in a niche in the center of the fountain in the garden
    just out of reach,
it stands as always, no oil inside it, but lit for the benefit of each
person born and meant to die.

So the barrel finally hits the bottom of Ni-
agara Falls and with a crack bursts its ironclad staves.
And the emptiness inside, filled with pure emptiness, flows out
    and disappears in the waves.

الله

# GLOSSARY

*al-hamdulillah wa shukrulillah*: Praise be to God, and thanks be to God

*as-salaam alaikum*: Peace be upon you (singular and plural)

*allahu akbar*: God is Great

*bismillah*: In the Name of God

*cadi*: A judge or arbiter between parties in conflict

*deen of Allah*: The Way (or life-transaction) of God (also: the religion of God)

*dhikr*: "Remembrance" of God, mantra-like invocation using repeated Divine Names or phrases

*diwan*: Gathering, as in a group of advisors or leaders

*hammam*: traditional steam and hot water bath house

*iman*: Faith, belief

*insha'Allah*: If God wills

*La howla wa la quwata ila billahi 'ali al-atheem*: No power and no strength but with Allah the Great

*la ilaha illa Allah*: There is no god but Allah (God)

*majlis*: A gathering

*malakut*: The spiritual and intellectual realm

*mulk*: The corporeal realm, the earthly sphere (literally "the kingdom")

*nafs*: Variously described as the lower self, the ego, that veil of our being which impedes wisdom

*Qâbel and Hâbel*: In the Qur'an, the Arabic names of Cain and Abel

*qibla*: The direction of prayer, toward Mecca

*salallahu alayhi wa salam*: Peace and blessings of Allah be upon him

*tasbih*: The Muslim and Sufi "rosary" of 99 beads for the Names of Allah

*wali, waliyya*: male and female Arabic for "friend" of God, or saintly person

*wazir* (or vizier): Advisor, King's or Sultan's "right hand man"

*wudhu*: The ritual washing before making salat (formal prayer)

*Ya Seen*: Sura 36 of the Qur'an, traditionally recited for someone who has died

*zakat*: 2.5% tax paid annually on yearly maintained wealth

# ABOUT THE AUTHOR

Born in 1940 in Oakland, California, Daniel Abdal-Hayy Moore's first book of poems, *Dawn Visions*, was published by Lawrence Ferlinghetti of City Lights Books, San Francisco, in 1964, and the second in 1972, *Burnt Heart/ Ode to the War Dead*. He created and directed *The Floating Lotus Magic Opera Company* in Berkeley, California in the late 60s, and presented two major productions, *The Walls Are Running Blood*, and *Bliss Apocalypse*. He became a Sufi Muslim in 1970, performed the Hajj in 1972, and lived and traveled throughout Morocco, Spain, Algeria and Nigeria, landing in California and publishing *The Desert is the Only Way Out*, and *Chronicles of Akhira* in the early 80s (Zilzal Press). Residing in Philadelphia since 1990, in 1996 he published *The Ramadan Sonnets* (Jusoor/City Lights), and in 2002, *The Blind Beekeeper* (Jusoor/Syracuse University Press). He has been the major editor for a number of works, including *The Burdah* of Shaykh Busiri, and *The Prayer of the Oppressed*, by Imam Nasir al-Dar'i, both translated by Shaykh Hamza Yusuf, and the poetry of Palestinian poet, Mahmoud Darwish, translated by Munir Akash. He is also widely published on the worldwide web: *The American Muslim, DeenPort*, and his own website and poetry blog, among others: *www.danielmoorepoetry.com, www.ecstaticxchange.wordpress. com*. He has also been poetry editor for *Seasons Journal*, and a new translation by Munir Akash of *State of Siege*, by Mahmoud Darwish, from Syracuse University Press. In 2011 he was a winner of the *Nazim Hikmet Prize for Poetry*. The Ecstatic Exchange Series is bringing out the extensive body of his works of poetry (a complete list of published works on page 2).

# POETIC WORKS by Daniel Abdal-Hayy Moore
## Published and Unpublished

Dawn Visions (published by City Lights, 1964)

Burnt Heart/Ode to the War Dead (published by City Lights, 1972)

This Body of Black Light Gone Through the Diamond (printed by Fred Stone, Cambridge, Mass, 1965)

On The Streets at Night Alone (1965?)

All Hail the Surgical Lamp (1967)

States of Amazement (1970)

---

Abdallah Jones and the Disappearing-Dust Caper (published by The Ecstatic Exchange/Crescent Series, 2006)

Ala-udeen & the Magic Lamp (published by The Ecstatic Exchange/ Crescent Series, 2011)

The Chronicles of Akhira (1981) (published by Zilzal Press with Typoglyphs by Karl Kempton, 1986) (published in Sparrow on the Prophet's Tomb, The Ecstatic Exchange, 2010)

Mouloud (1984) (A Zilzal Press chapbook, 1995) (published in Sparrow on the Prophet's Tomb, The Ecstatic Exchange, 2010)

Man is the Crown of Creation (1984)

The Look of the Lion (The Parabolas of Sight) (1984)

The Desert is the Only Way Out (completed 4/21/84) (Zilzal Press chapbook, 1985)

Atomic Dance (1984) (am here books, 1988)

Outlandish Tales (1984)

Awake as Never Before (12/26/84) (Zilzal Press chapbook, 1993)

Glorious Intervals (1/1/85) (Zilzal Press chapbook, ?)

Long Days on Earth/Book I (1/28 – 8/30/85)

Long Days on Earth/Book II (Hayy Ibn Yaqzan)

Long Days on Earth/Book III (1/22/86)

Long Days on Earth/Book IV (1986)

The Ramadan Sonnets (Long Days on Earth/Book V) (5/9 – 6/11/86) (published by Jusoor/City Lights Books, 1996) (Republished as Ramadan Sonnets by The Ecstatic Exchange, 2005)

Long Days on Earth/Book VI (6-8/30/86)

Holograms (9/4/86 – 3/26/87)

History of the World (The Epic of Man's Survival) (4/7 – 6/18/87)

Exploratory Odes (6/25 – 10/18/87)

The Man at the End of the World (11/11 – 12/10/87)

The Perfect Orchestra (3/30 – 7/25/88) (published by The Ecstatic Exchange, 2009)

Fed from Underground Springs (7/30 – 11/23/88)

Ideas of the Heart (11/27/88 – 5/5/89)

New Poems (scattered poems, out of series, from 3/24 – 8/9/89)

Facing Mecca (5/16 – 11/11/89)

A Maddening Disregard for the Passage of Time (11/17/89 – 5/20/90) (published by The Ecstatic Exchange, 2009)

The Heart Falls in Love with Visions of Perfection (6/15/90 – 6/2/91)

Like When You Wave at a Train and the Train Hoots Back at You (Farid's Book) (6/11 – 7/26/91) (published by The Ecstatic Exchange, 2008)

Orpheus Meets Morpheus (8/1/91– 3/14/92)

The Puzzle (3/21/92 – 8/17/93) (published by The Ecstatic Exchange, 2011)

The Greater Vehicle (10/17/93 – 4/30/94)

A Hundred Little 3-D Pictures (5/14/94 – 9/11/95)

The Angel Broadcast (9/29 – 12/17/95)

Mecca/Medina Time-Warp (12/19/95 – 1/6/96) (published as a Zilzal Press chapbook, 1996) (Published in Sparrow on the Prophet's Tomb, The Ecstatic Exchange, 2010)

Miracle Songs for the Millennium (1/20 – 10/16/96)

The Blind Beekeeper (11/15/96 – 5/30/97) (published 2002 by Jusoor/ Syracuse University Press)

Chants for the Beauty Feast (6/3 – 10/28/97) (published by The Ecstatic Exchange, 2011)

You Open a Door and it's a Starry Night (10/29/97 – 5/23/98) (published by The Ecstatic Exchange, 2009)

Salt Prayers (5/29 – 10/24/98) (published by The Ecstatic Exchange, 2005)

Some (10/25/98 – 4/25/99)

Flight to Egypt (5/1 – 5/16/99)

I Imagine a Lion (5/21 – 11/15/99) (published by The Ecstatic Exchange, 2006)

Millennial Prognostications (11/25/99 – 2/2/2000) (published by the Ecstatic Exchange, 2009)

Shaking the Quicksilver Pool (2/4 – 10/8/2000) (published by The Ecstatic Exchange, 2009)

Blood Songs (10/9/2000 – 4/3/2001)

The Music Space (4/10 – 9/16/2001) (published by The Ecstatic Exchange, 2007)

Where Death Goes (9/20/2001 – 5/1/2002) (published by The Ecstatic Exchange, 2009)

The Flame of Transformation Turns to Light (99 Ghazals Written in English) (5/14 – 8/21/2002) (Published by The Ecstatic Exchange, 2007)

Through Rose-Colored Glasses (7/22/2002 – 1/15/2003) (published by The Ecstatic Exchange, 2007)

Psalms for the Broken-Hearted (1/22 – 5/25/2003) (published by The Ecstatic Exchange, 2006)

Hoopoe's Argument (5/27 – 9/18/03)

Love is a Letter Burning in a High Wind (9/21 – 11/6/2003) (published by The Ecstatic Exchange, 2006)

Laughing Buddha/Weeping Sufi (11/7/2003 – 1/10/2004) (published by The Ecstatic Exchange, 2005)

Mars and Beyond (1/20 – 3/29/2004) (published by The Ecstatic Exchange, 2005)

Underwater Galaxies (4/5 – 7/21/2004) (published by The Ecstatic Exchange, 2007)

Cooked Oranges (7/23/2004 – 1/24/2005 (published by The Ecstatic Exchange, 2007)

Holiday from the Perfect Crime (1/25 – 6/11/2005) (published by The Ecstatic Exchange, 2011)

Stories Too Fiery to Sing Too Watery to Whisper (6/13 – 10/24/2005)

Coattails of the Saint (10/26/2005 – 5/10/2006 ) (published by The Ecstatic Exchange, 2006)

In the Realm of Neither (5/14/2006 – 11/12/06) (published by The Ecstatic Exchange, 2008)

Invention of the Wheel (11/13/06 – 6/10/07) (published by The Ecstatic Exchange, 2010)

The Sound of Geese Over the House (6/15 – 11/4/07)

The Fire Eater's Lunchbreak (11/11/07 – 5/19/2008) (published by The Ecstatic Exchange, 2008)

Sparks Off the Main Strike (5/24/2008 – 1/10/2009) (published by The Ecstatic Exchange, 2010)

Stretched Out on Amethysts (1/13 – 9/17/2009) (published by The Ecstatic Exchange, 2010)

The Throne Perpendicular to All that is Horizontal (9/18/09 – 1/25/10)

In Constant Incandescence (2/10 – 8/13/10) (published by The Ecstatic Exchange, 2011)

The Caged Bear Spies the Angel (8/30/10 –3/6/11) (published by The Ecstatic Exchange, 2011)

This Light Slants Upward (3/7/11 – 10/13/11)

Ramadan is Burnished Sunlight (part of This Light Slants Upward, published separately by The Ecstatic Exchange, 2011)

The Match That Becomes a Conflagration (10/14/11 – )

www.ingramcontent.com/pod-product-compliance
Lightning Source LLC
Chambersburg PA
CBHW051840040426
42447CB00006B/632